Classroom Literature Circles
for Primary Grades

Grades K-2

by Elizabeth Suarez Aguerre

Carson-Dellosa Publishing Company, Inc.

Greensboro, North Carolina

Dedication

To P.

Credits

Editor
Kelly Gunzenhauser

Layout Design
Van Harris

Cover Design
Matthew Van Zomeren

Cover Photographs
© 2001 Brand X Pictures
© 2001 EyeWire, Inc. All rights reserved.
© Photodisc

Printed in the USA • All rights reserved.   ISBN 1-59441-247-2

Table of Contents

Chapter 1

Literature Circles
What are they and why should teachers use them?

What are literature circles?

The use of literature circles has been defined as a "strategy for," an "approach to," and a "method of" teaching literature. Regardless of the terms used, literature circles, quite simply, are small groups of students who read the same book and gather on a regular basis to discuss their reading. The purpose of literature circles, then, is to have students discuss, respond to, and think about real literature. Even emerging readers can participate in and benefit from literature circles in the classroom. Literature circles expose developing readers to many critical reading strategies and behaviors, such as responding to and interacting with text, finding the main idea, working with vocabulary, developing opinions about literature, sharing reactions, and generating and answering literature-based comprehension questions. Literature circle activities often require higher-order thinking, a critical component of being a successful reader. Many teachers tend to wait until students are older, or "more ready," to introduce cooperative activities like literature circles. However, young students develop and grow as readers *because* of exposure to such activities.

Literature circles can be incorporated into an existing primary reading program with minimal effort and maximum benefits. Your job is to set up the classroom literature circle systems and to ensure that students are discussing the story and thinking about the literature. You will be surprised at how natural this is for young children! Emerging and developing readers instinctively want to share, discuss, and talk about the stories they read. The great thing about literature circles is that although you still direct students and keep them focused so that they end up right where you want them, it is the students who do the thinking, writing and drawing, discussing, debating, and sharing. This book demonstrates how to be a guide and facilitator as young students develop their reading responses, learn to make connections with text, form opinions, and realize the impact literature can have. It also details the procedure for introducing and implementing a literature circle system in kindergarten through second-grade classrooms, provides reproducible student role forms for literature circle activities, and offers strategies and additional reproducibles for specific situations.

This Chapter Includes:
- a description of the literature circle method
- an introduction to the roles
- a description and scenario of a literature circle classroom
- information about why the use of literature circles is an effective way for very young students to study literature

Who can use literature circles?

Literature circles have traditionally been used in intermediate classrooms because older students are more independent. It is a myth, however, that literature circles do not work in primary-level classrooms. Quite the contrary! It is often said that young children are like sponges—they absorb everything to which they are exposed. Primary literature circles are no exception. In addition, they are simple to implement and amazingly effective. Emerging readers will also benefit greatly from being in cooperative groups that discuss literature because in later grades, when this is a much more common practice, they will already have had years of experience.

Although many school-age children are already familiar with the concept of working in a group from the "circle time" structure used in preschool, it does take longer to "train" kindergartners to do literature circles than second graders. Children do not instinctively know and understand that literature can make them think and feel things, or that good readers develop questions and ideas while reading. They do not know many of the strategies that proficient readers naturally use while reading to make the experience more rewarding and to help them understand the text. Literature circles expose young children to the strategies and behaviors that they need for future educational success. With practice, developing readers can respond independently to literature and can even interact to share or debate their opinions.

What are the major components of literature circles?

The major components of literature circles are books, role forms, and students. Literature circle discussions are based on in-class readings of the selected books. Each student is assigned a role form to complete after the day's reading. The student then uses the completed form as a guide during the after-reading discussion. Many of these role forms help students think about and discuss critical literary elements, such as characters, plot, and vocabulary. The forms can also be used to assess reading comprehension.

This book includes two types of role forms. The first type is labeled as Level 1–Basic. These forms cover simple but critical skills for beginning readers and are appropriate for students in kindergarten through first grade, prewriters, and ESL students. The second type of role form is labeled Level 2–Traditional, and it requires students to evaluate or respond on a higher level. These forms are appropriate for second graders and for any younger students who can complete basic writing and critical thinking tasks. Level 2 forms are more similar to the traditional literature circle role forms used with older students. Select the particular forms that match your students' levels. The important thing is that role forms require each student to respond to the story in some way and then share that response in his group.

What are the student roles covered in this book?

Level 1–Basic:
- My Favorite Part (page 17)—The student draws and writes about his favorite part of the story.
- I Want to Share (page 18)—The student draws a picture and writes about one thing from the story that she wants to share.
- Reader's Journal Response (page 19)—On a journal page, the student responds to the story using drawings and/or writing.
- Liked/Did Not Like (page 20)—The student uses pictures and/or words to complete a chart telling what he did and did not like about the story.
- New Book Cover (page 21)—The student creates a new book cover for the story.
- The Story Made Me Feel . . . (page 22)—The student completes a chart about how the story made her feel.
- Book Review (page 23)—The student writes a book review to recommend it (or not) to a friend.
- My Opinion (page 24)—The student uses a variety of adjectives to describe and explain his opinion of the book.

Level 2–Traditional:
- Story Summarizer (pages 25-28)—The student summarizes the day's reading and reviews the summary during the group discussion.
- Question Creator (pages 29-32)—The student creates questions and answers for the group to discuss.
- Imaginative Illustrator (pages 33-36)—The student selects part of the story to illustrate and shares the illustration with the group.
- Word Watcher (pages 37-40)—The student defines story vocabulary to discuss with the group.
- Bridge Builder (pages 41-43)—The student makes personal connections between the story and his own life.

There are a variety of forms for each role in the Level 2 section. For example, there are four different **Story Summarizer** forms. The forms for each role vary in difficulty; they are ordered from easiest to most difficult. Select the form for each role that best suits students' needs and abilities.

Additionally, there are two levels of **Circle Supervisor** role forms (pages 44-45). The Circle Supervisor's job is to guide the group throughout the literature circle discussion and ensure that the group work runs smoothly. One form is more advanced than the other. As with the other forms, select the Circle Supervisor form that best suits that student's abilities and needs.

What does a literature circles classroom look like?

Until you see literature circles in action, it can be difficult to understand how the components come together. This section will help you "get it." There are three chunks of time spent during a session: reading and role form completion time, group discussion time, and whole-class discussion time. Following are two descriptions of what the process looks like when students know the system. The first scenario describes a kindergarten classroom with emerging readers. The second scenario depicts a second-grade classroom with developing and advanced readers.

Scenario #1:

The kindergarten students in Mrs. Aguerre's classroom have been using *The Very Hungry Caterpillar* by Eric Carle (Philomel Books, 1994) for literature circle activities. Mrs. Aguerre announces, "Today we will do literature circles with *The Very Hungry Caterpillar*." She reminds students to sit in their literature circle groups. Because it is still early in the school year and many of Mrs. Aguerre's students are emerging readers, she is using role forms from the Level 1–Basic section. Mrs. Aguerre has introduced new forms as students progress and develop. At this point, students are familiar with four of the forms: My Favorite Part, I Want To Share, Reader's Journal Response, and Liked/Did Not Like. Therefore, students in each group have four different role forms to share. Mrs. Aguerre refers to the literature circle pocket chart, which has pockets labeled with these role names. Students' names are on index cards that rotate from pocket to pocket. After answering questions and ensuring that each student knows his role for the day, Mrs. Aguerre rereads *The Very Hungry Caterpillar*. Since students have been working with the story for a few days, they know the text and are prepared to do literature circles with it.

After hearing the story read aloud, students begin to independently work on their assigned role forms. Mrs. Aguerre moves around the room, stopping occasionally to help a student answer a question, prompt another to work more quickly, or remind someone else to slow down and check her work. After a few minutes, Mrs. Aguerre tells the class that role form completion time is almost up, so students should complete their forms quickly.

When she calls students together for group sharing time, students put down their pencils and crayons and look to the other group members. Each group's Circle Supervisor leads group members in taking turns to share their role forms. During the discussion, Mrs. Aguerre circulates through the classroom and joins different groups. She sees one group listening intently as one of their members, Lance, shares what he liked and did not like about the story. A minor debate ensues as two group members disagree with his choices. Mrs. Aguerre reminds the group to use positive language. She prompts Stephanie, a group member, to say, "I don't agree with you because I think . . ." instead of, "That's wrong!" Mrs. Aguerre joins another group in which students are sharing their favorite parts of the story.

After several minutes, Mrs. Aguerre calls time, and students return to the whole-class setting. A few students share their thoughts about the day's literature circles. Mrs. Aguerre holds a question-and-answer session to clear up any confusion, shares positive observations, and gives suggestions for next time.

Scenario #2:

The second-grade students in Mr. Armstrong's classroom have been reading the novel *Freckle Juice* by Judy Blume (Yearling, 1978). Mr. Armstrong announces, "Today we will be doing literature circles with the second chapter." Because Mr. Armstrong's students have been participating in literature circles for some time and many of them are reading at or above grade level, he has been using the five Level 2–Traditional role forms. To ensure that students know their literature circle roles for the day, he refers to the literature circle pocket chart, which has pockets labeled with the names of the roles. Students' names are on index cards that rotate from pocket to pocket.

After answering questions, Mr. Armstrong sits at his desk and silently reads the day's chapter while students independently do the same. (Mr. Armstrong usually reads the entire book before starting the unit, then reads a second time along with students in order to model reading for them.)

After a reasonable amount of time, Mr. Armstrong tells students that they should be finishing their reading and beginning to work on their role forms. Students who are working too slowly or too quickly adjust their pace. Mr. Armstrong circulates, pausing occasionally to help a student, as some students finish their role forms and take their pencils, completed role forms, and books to their meeting locations. (For other activities these "early birds" can do, see pages 73–74.) Their movement prompts students who are still working to finish their role forms and meet the group members who are waiting to begin the discussion.

When all groups are assembled, each group's Circle Supervisor, whose responsibility it is to keep order, leads group members as they take turns reviewing and discussing the role forms. Since the real purpose of the role forms is to spark discussions and debates about the literature, many students are actively participating without referring to their forms. Fortunately, the Circle Supervisors' jobs are minimal since students are experienced in literature circles and advancing nicely.

During the discussion, Mr. Armstrong walks around and joins different groups. He sees one group flipping through their books looking for a particular scene and debating about why a character did something. Half of the group members disagree with the others about the cause of the character's actions. The Circle Supervisor reminds her classmates to take turns while they attempt to convince each other. Mr. Armstrong moves on to observe another group that is sharing the different ways in which a particular event in the day's reading reminded them of events from their own lives.

At the end of the allotted time, Mr. Armstrong calls time and students return to the whole-class setting. A few students discuss their thoughts about the day's literature circles and share some of the positive and negative things that happened within their groups. Mr. Armstrong holds another question-and-answer session, and students discuss suggestions for improving their experiences for next time.

Obviously, in addition to the types of role forms, there are differences between the kindergarten and second-grade scenarios. For example, the kindergartners were already in their groups at the very beginning of the session, whereas the second graders read and completed the role forms at their seats, then moved to their assigned locations. The kindergartners' teacher read aloud to them while the second graders read independently. Group discussions were also more advanced in the second-grade scenario. These simple modifications help groups of younger readers function more effectively while the outcomes are still the same: students respond to, interact with, and think about literature in a cooperative setting.

Why should a teacher use literature circles in a primary classroom?

The previous scenes show what literature circles look like in action, but why should a teacher use this particular approach to teach reading and critical thinking? There is much research to support the general use of literature circles, and many teachers have seen the positive outcomes of using this method with young students.

Researchers have found that the use of literature circles:
- allows students "to practice authentic reading behaviors" and sparks student interest through peer enthusiasm (Hollingsworth, 1998)
- invites students to actively participate in sharing their ideas and building meaning from what they read (Daniels, 1994)
- dramatically changes students' attitudes toward books and reading (Samway, Whang, Cade, et al., 1991)
- engages reluctant readers and helps them feel more confident (Samway, Whang, Cade, et al., 1991; Samway and Whang, 1996)
- increases "talk" about books both in and out of the classroom (Samway, Whang, Cade, et al., 1991)
- helps students understand themselves and others through personal connections made with characters and story themes (Samway, Whang, Cade, et al., 1991)
- allows students of all levels and abilities to succeed (Moen, 2000)
- helps students develop cooperative learning and social skills (Moen, 2000)
- helps emerging readers develop cognitively, orally, and socially (Daniels, 1994)

Teachers have found that the use of literature circles helps emerging and primary readers:
- develop reading skills
- practice authentic reading strategies
- learn to recognize story patterns and elements
- select a larger number of books for independent reading
- complete in-class reading more efficiently
- become more interested in and enthusiastic about reading
- develop social skills while working with others

All about Roles and Role Forms

Along with books and students, roles are a critical component of literature circles. Teach this information thoroughly because student role forms are the guides for circle discussions. It would be wonderful if teachers could just tell students to "talk about the book," but many young children are not capable of such an open-ended assignment. With very young emerging readers, the role forms can be more simplistic, but can still keep students focused and give them topics to talk about in their groups. Although there are basic, critical elements students need to cover (such as characters, vocabulary, etc.) when responding to literature, the possibilities for role forms are endless. In addition to the choices you have in this chapter, you might decide to create your own role forms.

This Chapter Includes:
- reproducible role forms for all Level 1 and Level 2 roles
- a description of each role
- tips for assigning role forms to students
- special instructions for the Circle Supervisor role (both levels)

This chapter consists primarily of reproducible student role forms. There are two role form sections: Level 1–Basic (pages 17–24) and Level 2–Traditional (pages 25-43). Level 1 forms are very basic and cover simple (but still critical) skills for beginning readers. They allow emerging readers to practice interacting with and responding to text. They also give students information to share during circle time. These forms are more appropriate for very young children or students who are still struggling with reading. The Level 1 forms are a bit "friendlier" and less intimidating for students whose teachers are concerned about doing literature circles with primary students.

Level 2 forms are more advanced and require students to evaluate or respond on a higher level. These forms are more similar to the traditional literature circle role forms that are often used with older students. They can also be used with younger students who are capable readers and writers and who are ready for more of a challenge. These forms have several versions for each role. They are arranged in order from easiest to most difficult.

Each role form varies in complexity and in how much time it takes for students to complete. There are easier forms for students who are emerging or struggling readers and harder forms for advanced students. So, it is easy to select the particular forms that best match students' levels and needs. All of the role forms require each student to respond to the story in some way and then share that response in his group. Of course, students must first be taught how to complete and use the role forms within their literature circles. Once students know how to use the role forms, you are free to participate, observe, and assess.

Level 1–Basic

This form is a powerful tool for children who naturally want to share which parts of the story were their favorites and why. It is a simple way to help young students interact with and respond to text. Each student completing this role form draws a picture of her favorite part of the story in the box and then writes about it. (Very young students may benefit from a mini-lesson about what "favorite" means. Let students share which foods, movies, colors, etc., they like most. Explain that these are their favorites—favorite foods, favorite movies, and favorite colors.) This form can also be adapted in a number of ways for emerging readers. For example, students can dictate their writing to volunteers or older students. Students can also use invented spelling or copy words and phrases written on the board during a previous activity. A student who cannot write at all may simply skip the writing portion.

This role form requires the student to draw a picture of something he would like to share with his group and then write about his picture. It is similar in format to My Favorite Part but is more open-ended, allowing the student to respond to any aspect of the story. The student may choose to share his favorite part, but he may also share a part he thought was funny, something he found confusing, how the story was similar to something he had experienced, etc. Very young children may struggle a bit with the expectations for this form if they are not familiar with responding to a story; however, they will quickly understand it once you model and teach the form. When doing so, reread a familiar story aloud. Then, tell students that good readers often want to talk about stories after they read them. Brainstorm a web of ideas that readers might want to share, such as parts they liked or disliked, a part that reminded them of something in their own lives, something that was funny or confusing, etc. Then, use the I Want to Share form to share your own thoughts about the book. Think aloud as you draw a picture and then write about it. For example, if you just read *The Very Hungry Caterpillar* by Eric Carle (Philomel Books, 1994), you might say that the story reminded you of a time you felt sick because you ate too much. Then, draw a picture of yourself eating and looking ill and add a simple sentence beneath the picture. Model this process several times with different types of thoughts inspired by the same story. If necessary, adapt this form so that it does not require students to write, or let them use invented spelling or dictation to share their ideas.

Reader's Journal Response

This form is open-ended, asking students to respond to any aspect of the story. Students who have completed journal-type response activities in class will have no trouble with this form. It requires students to write and/or draw about the story. It might be helpful to explain that a journal is like a diary, except that students will write about what they read. Students who are assigned this form should be comfortable with some writing, either copying from the board or using invented spelling. It can also be helpful to have an adult volunteer assist students with the form, either by taking dictation or assisting with spelling and word selection.

Liked/Did Not Like

This form helps emerging readers develop and defend opinions about the text. The student completes a chart using words and/or pictures describing what he liked and did not like about the story. Once students are comfortable with using this form (or if you are already working with more advanced readers), it is a good idea to require the student to explain why he liked or did not like each aspect of the story about which he has chosen to write. This is an easy way for students to begin to develop the very important skills of elaborating and supporting their points of view.

New Book Cover

This form allows the student to express her creativity by designing a new book cover for the story. Students will enjoy the artistic aspect of this form, and it will help them recognize and internalize the format of a book cover: title, author(s) and illustrator(s), and a design that gives clues about the main idea of the story. If you tell a student to draw one picture that represents the story, often she will draw the main idea without assistance. Therefore, you can also use this form to spark a discussion about main idea.

The Story Made Me Feel...

This form requires the student to complete a chart explaining which parts of the story made him feel amused, happy, sad, mad, or confused. This form will help young students realize that literature can actually make them feel different emotions. It will also help emerging readers develop the ability to make personal connections with literature.

Book Review ★★★★

This form requires the student to form an opinion about the book and decide whether she would recommend it to a friend. The student must then explain why she thinks a friend would or would not like the book. The form also includes a space for her to draw a picture to further explain her opinion. By completing this form, students are tackling an early form of persuasive writing.

This form requires the student to select adjectives to describe the story. It is therefore more appropriate for students who are capable of using only writing to share their thoughts. A student chooses a few adjectives, such as silly, scary, confusing, etc., from a word box and explains why he thinks those words describe the story. Students may also dictate their opinions and reasons to an adult volunteer or older student.

Level 2–Traditional

The Story Summarizer's job is to summarize the day's reading using one of four different forms. Form #1 requires the student to draw a picture to show what the story was about and also provides lines for the student to write a sentence or two about his picture. Form #2 requires the student to summarize the story using illustrations to show what happened first, next, and last. Form #3 provides prompts to help each student summarize the story in paragraph form. Form #4 requires the student to summarize the story using a "Somebody-Wanted-But-So Then" chart on which he fills out the character, goal, problem, and solution. Regardless of the form used, when the Story Summarizer shares in his literature circle, he should retell the story while referring to his completed form.

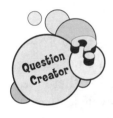

The Question Creator's job is to create questions and answers about the story for other students in her literature circle to answer. The students should try to think like teachers who write questions for students. This role form may take more time for students to understand. Some of the forms provide more guidance than others, but all provide some support for primary students. Form #1 is simple and more appropriate for a struggling reader because it allows the student to illustrate the answer rather than write about it. First, the student must write a question she has after reading or listening to the story. Then, she may draw her answer. Form #2 requires writing but also provides students with guidance and support. The questions are partially written, and the student only needs to fill in the blanks to finish the questions. Form #3 provides support in the form of the "Five Ws" (and "One H"): Who, What, When, Where, Why, and How. The student should think of six questions, one that begins with each word. Form #4 is not very structured. It requires the Question Creator to make up and answer two questions but suggests that the questions be "thinking questions." Model completing the form to show students the difference between an "easy" or "no thinking" question such as, "What color was the character's shirt?" and a "thinking question" such as, "Why do you think the character did that?" When the Question Creator shares in her literature circle, she should read the question she created and allow her group members to answer it, using the book if necessary. After the group members have answered the question, the Question Creator should read her own answer in order to agree or disagree with her group members' answers. This often leads to healthy debates!

The Imaginative Illustrator's job is to visualize and illustrate parts from the story—an important, but often overlooked, reading strategy. Students respond well to being told that they have "Brain TVs" in their heads; they should "see" everything that occurs in the reading—they should see action in their minds, much as they would on a TV screen. Even when using picture books with primary students, it is important to help students realize that they should not rely solely on the illustrations provided in books. Having students draw what they see in their heads helps them to internalize visualization as a natural reading strategy, a useful skill when they "graduate" to novels and chapter books with few or no illustrations. Form #1 simply tells the student to illustrate a scene from the story, then explain to the group why he drew that particular scene. Form #2 is similar to the first, but also requires a student to write why he drew that particular scene. Form #3 is useful for students who have difficulty departing from the book's illustrations. It asks the student to picture himself in the story and draw himself in a scene from the book. The student cannot simply copy one of the book's illustrations because it must be changed in some way. Form #4 also instructs the student to draw a picture of the story with himself in it, but then has the student write about whether he is a character or his usual self. The form asks whether he does the same things the characters are doing or if his presence changes something in the story. This form requires more creativity and a higher level of thinking. Regardless of the form used, the Imaginative Illustrator should share his illustration and reasoning with his group. Then, the group members should comment and ask questions.

The Word Watcher's job is to find and define vocabulary words from the story. The words can be selected by students or the teacher, depending on whether students are ready to choose words they think are interesting or important, or whether there are certain words from the story you want to teach. (Only Form #2 exclusively features student-selected words.) Note that definitions can be created by students, taken from a dictionary, or can evolve from a class discussion. Form #1 requires the student to copy four words from the story and draw their meanings in the boxes. Form #2 instructs the student to select words and then complete a chart by writing each word, a sentence from the story using the word, the reason she chose the word, and what she thinks it might mean. This form gives much more responsibility to the student because it allows her to both choose the word and define it. Form #3 is a word web that requires a student to write a word, a synonym, an antonym, and a new sentence using the word. The form can be adapted for prewriters by requiring them to draw inside the web. Form #4 requires the student to complete two word charts in which she must copy the word and its sentence from the story, write its definition, and write a new sentence using the word. Before assigning this form, determine whether the student should use a dictionary, a class-created definition, or context clues. Regardless of the form used, when sharing in her group, the Word Watcher should first read the sentences containing the word from the story and ask group members what they think the word means. After the group discusses the word, the Word Watcher can continue sharing her answers.

The Bridge Builder's job is to make a personal connection, or "bridge," between the story and his own life. Students can truly interact with literature by bringing their own experiences and prior knowledge to their reading. Form #1 requires the student to draw a picture and write about how the story reminded him of his own life. Form #2 requires more specific writing but provides support for students by requiring them to fill in blanks in sentences (such as "The character _____ from the story reminds me of _____ because _____."). After filling in the blanks for three sentences, the student may draw a picture to go with each. Form #3 is very open-ended and unstructured; it simply provides a journal page format for a student to write and/or draw something of which the story reminded him. When the Bridge Builder shares in his circle, he should first revisit the relevant section of the story with his group. Then, he should share his personal connections and ask group members to share any personal connections of their own.

Each group is "supervised" by a Circle Supervisor. In addition to completing a role form and participating in the discussion, the Circle Supervisor ensures that the group is functioning efficiently and communicating in a positive manner. As students become more comfortable with the roles in their groups, the Circle Supervisor's job becomes almost nonexistent because students know what is expected of them and they want to participate. With good Circle Supervisors in place, your role in facilitating the groups becomes less critical. The Circle Supervisor form should be introduced to all students before they meet in their literature circle groups. Form #1 (Level 1) has less text, includes more graphics, and has simple tips for staying on task and working cooperatively within the group. Form #2 (Level 2) has more text and provides tips for guiding the group's discussion, including examples of wording that is appropriate to use within the circles.

Assigning Role Forms to Students

As you assign role forms to students based on their needs and reading levels, there are several things to consider when choosing the role form assignments. Your first consideration is whether you will be selecting from the Level 1–Basic forms or Level 2–Traditional forms. Although Level 1 forms are appropriate for young children and emerging readers, you may also want to start with these forms if you are teaching developing second graders or introducing students to literature circles for the first time.

The Level 2 forms are more advanced and more challenging. They also vary in difficulty so that some younger students can use them, as well. Select the forms that utilize skills your students already have or can learn. For example, if you have been teaching summarizing and students are becoming proficient in that skill, assign the easier Level 2 Story Summarizer form, but select the remaining roles from the Level 1 section.

The next step is to decide whether all students in one group will use the same form or different forms. For example, if you have chosen to use the Level 1 forms, you must then decide if you want to have a group of students in which every student is completing, sharing, and discussing the same My Favorite Part role form; or if students are ready, you might prefer to have students in the group use different forms, such as My Favorite Part, I Want to Share, Question Creator, etc. It is often a good idea for each group to use the same forms at first, so that students become comfortable with each role. If you begin in this manner, you can then allow group members to have different roles.

Role forms should be assigned after you have determined the texts that will be used and the group assignments. These processes are discussed thoroughly in Chapter 3, "Getting Literature Circles Going in the Classroom" (page 46). Evaluating or assessing the execution of role forms on a regular basis will demonstrate which students need more help with the process or the reading, and which students are ready to advance to more difficult role forms.

My Favorite Part

Name _____

Date _____

◯◯◯◯◯◯◯◯◯◯◯◯

Title of Story _____

Draw a picture of your favorite part of the story.

My favorite part was _____

_____

_____

_____

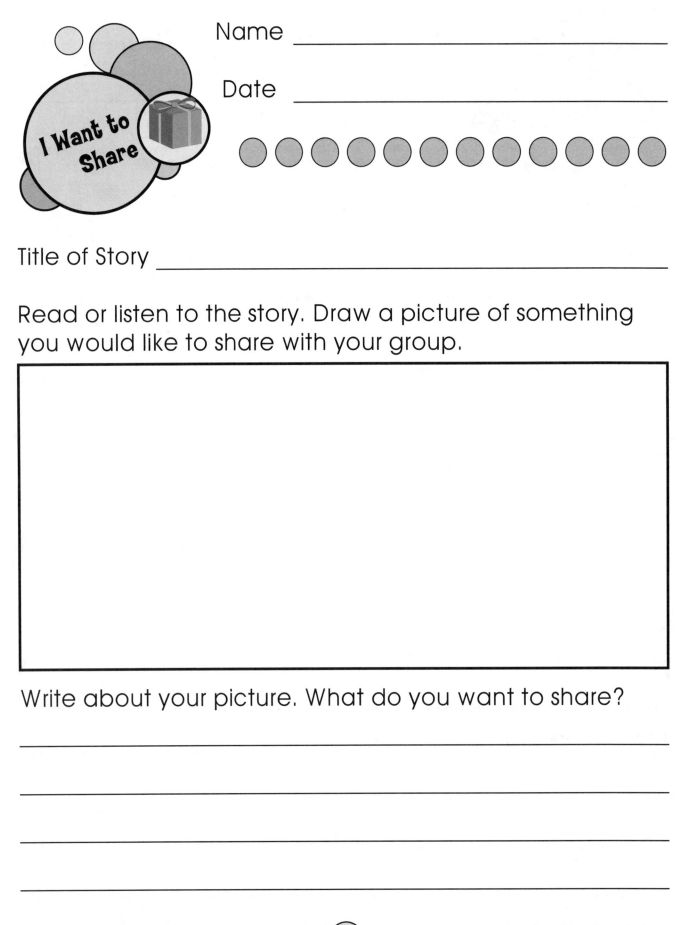

I Want to Share

Name _____

Date _____

Title of Story _____

Read or listen to the story. Draw a picture of something you would like to share with your group.

Write about your picture. What do you want to share?

_____

_____

_____

Reader's Journal Response

Name _____

Date _____

◯ ◯ ◯ ◯ ◯ ◯ ◯ ◯ ◯ ◯ ◯ ◯

Title of Story _____

Write about what you read. Draw a picture of the story in the box.

_____

_____

_____

_____

_____

_____

_____

_____

_____

_____

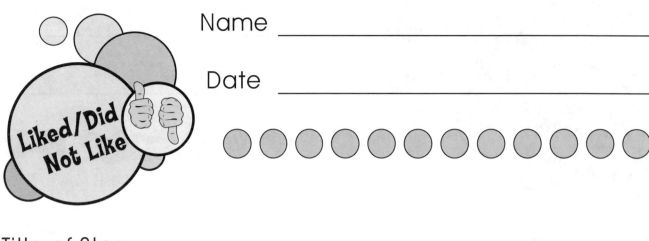

Name _____

Date _____

Liked/Did Not Like

Title of Story _____

Share what you liked and did not like about the story. You can use words and pictures in your chart.

What I Liked about the Story	What I Did Not Like about the Story

Name _____

Date _____

Title of Story _____

Create a new book cover for the story. Write the title and the names of the author(s) and illustrator(s). Draw a picture that would make someone want to read the book.

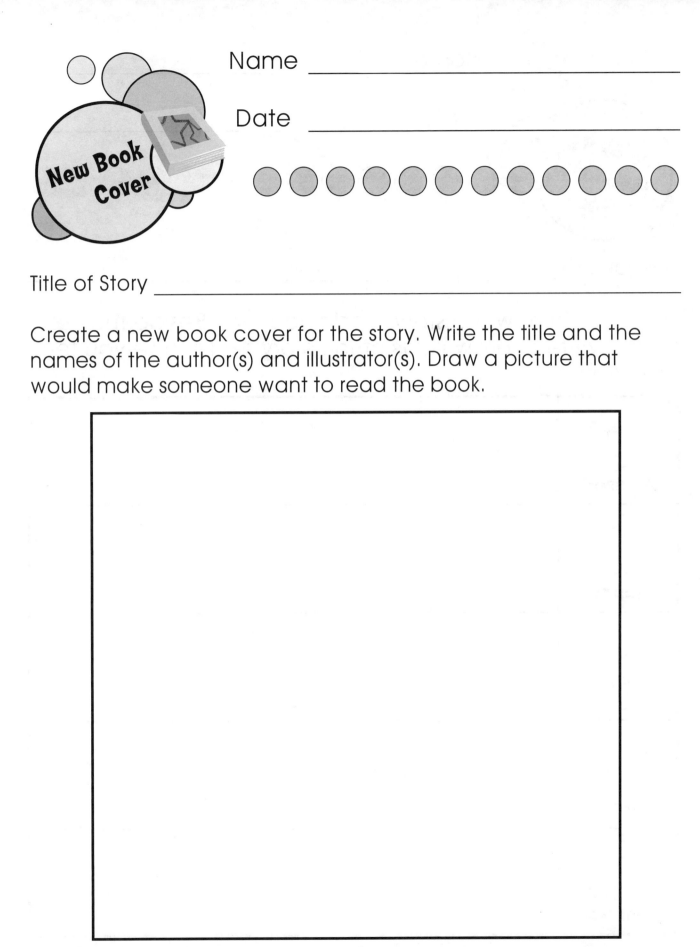

The Story Made Me Feel…

Name _____

Date _____

Title of Story _____

Think about how the story made you feel. Beside the words, write or draw parts of the story that made you feel that way.

Amused	
Happy	
Sad	
Mad	
Confused	

Book Review ★★★★

Name _____

Date _____

Write the title and name of the author(s). Circle the words <u>liked</u> or <u>did not like</u>. Write if you would tell a friend to read it. Draw a picture about what you wrote.

Title of Story _____

Author(s) _____

I liked/did not like this book. I think you would agree!

Here is why: _____

_____

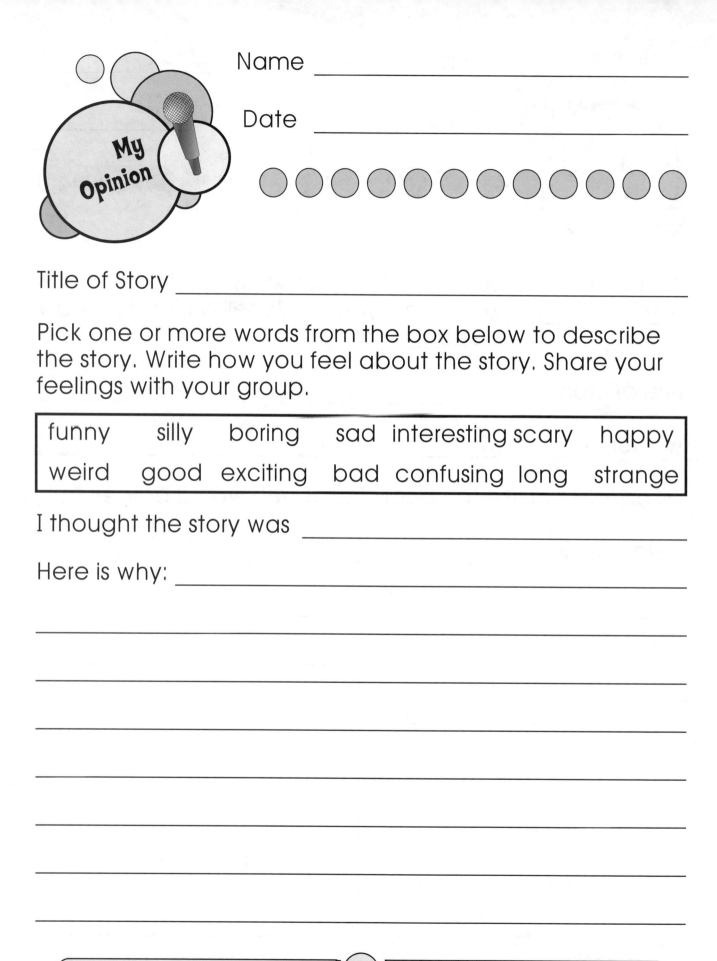

Name _____

Date _____

My Opinion

Title of Story _____

Pick one or more words from the box below to describe the story. Write how you feel about the story. Share your feelings with your group.

funny	silly	boring	sad	interesting	scary	happy
weird	good	exciting	bad	confusing	long	strange

I thought the story was _____

Here is why: _____

_____

_____

_____

_____

_____

_____

Story Summarizer

1 of 4

○ ○ ○ ○ ○ ○ ○ ○ ○ ○ ○ ○

Title of Story _____

Your job is to summarize the story. Read or listen to the story and draw a picture to show what it was about.

Write about your picture. What do you want to share with your group?

_____

_____

_____

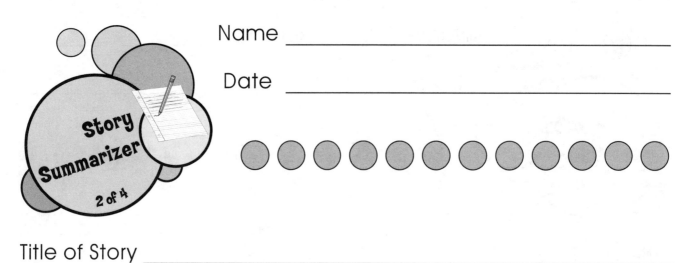

Name _____

Date _____

Title of Story _____

Your job is to summarize the story. Read or listen to the story. Fill in the chart below. Use the chart to help you share with your group.

Draw a picture to show what happened FIRST in the story.	
Draw a picture to show what happened NEXT in the story.	
Draw a picture to show what happened LAST in the story.	

Name _____

Date _____

⬤ ⬤ ⬤ ⬤ ⬤ ⬤ ⬤ ⬤ ⬤ ⬤ ⬤

Title of Story _____

Your job is to summarize the story. Read or listen to the story. Write four sentences to tell what the story was about. Share this form with your group.

The story was about _____

_____

_____

_____

First, _____

_____

_____

Next, _____

_____

_____

Last, _____

_____

_____

Name _____

Date _____

Story Summarizer

4 of 4

○ ○ ○ ○ ○ ○ ○ ○ ○ ○ ○ ○

Title of Story _____

Your job is to summarize the story. Read or listen to the story. Fill in the chart below. Use the chart when you share with your group.

Somebody (Character/s)	
Wanted (Goal)	
But (Problem)	
So Then (Solution)	

Name _____

Date _____

○○○○○○○○○○○○

Title of Story _____

Your job is to write a question about the story for your group to answer. Read or listen to the story. Think of a question. Draw your answer in the box.

My question: _____

_____

_____

_____

Name _____

Date _____

Title of Story _____

Your job is to write questions about the story for your group to answer. Read or listen to the story. Use the question starters below to help you write three questions. Write the answers to your questions.

1. Why do you think _____

_____

Answer: _____

_____

2. How do you think the character _____ felt when ___

_____

Answer: _____

_____

3. If you were _____ in the story, what would you do?

Answer: _____

_____

Name _____

Date _____

Title of Story _____

Your job is to write questions about the story for your group to answer. Pretend that you are the teacher. Read or listen to the story. Write your questions on the lines below. Answer the questions on the back of this page.

1. Who _____

_____

2. What _____

_____

3. When _____

_____

4. Where _____

_____

5. Why _____

_____

6. How _____

_____

Name _____

Date _____

Title of Story _____

Your job is to write questions about the story for your group to answer. Read or listen to the story. Think of some important questions. Write the questions and answers on the lines below. Remember to write "Thinking questions."

Question #1: _____

_____

_____

Answer: _____

_____

_____

Question #2: _____

_____

_____

Answer: _____

_____

_____

Name _____

Date _____

Title of Story _____

Your job is to choose a part of the story to draw for your group. Close your eyes and imagine part of the story on your "Brain TV." Draw it in the box below. Share your drawing with your group. Tell them why you chose that part to draw.

Name _____

Date _____

Title of Story _____

Your job is to choose a part of the story to draw for your group. Close your eyes. Imagine part of the story on your "Brain TV." Draw it in the box below. Write why you chose to draw that part. Share your drawing and writing with your group.

Why did you choose that part of the story to draw? _____

_____

_____

Name _____

Date _____

Title of Story _____

Your job is to choose a part of the story to draw—with you in it! Close your eyes. Imagine yourself in the story. Draw a picture of yourself in the story.

Name _____

Date _____

Title of Story _____

Your job is to choose a part of the story to draw—with you in it! Close your eyes. Imagine seeing yourself in the story. Draw a picture of yourself in the story.

Are you a character in the story or just yourself? Are you doing the same things as the characters? Are you changing something in the story? On the lines below, write about your drawing.

_____

_____

_____

Name _____

Date _____

⬤ ⬤ ⬤ ⬤ ⬤ ⬤ ⬤ ⬤ ⬤ ⬤ ⬤ ⬤

Title of Story _____

Your job is to draw the meanings of words from the story. Copy a word from the story on each blank line. Draw its meaning in the box.

_____	_____
_____	_____

Name _____

Date _____

Title of Story _____

Your job is to find special words from the story. Read or
listen to the story. Look for words that are interesting,
strange, hard, fun, or new. Write each word in a box and
fill in the chart below.

Word	Sentence from the Story	Why I Chose This Word	What I Think the Word Means

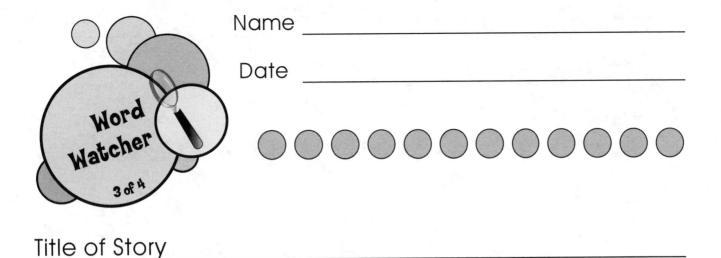

Title of Story _____

Your job is to define a word from the story. Read or listen to the story. Write the word in the circle below. Finish the word web.

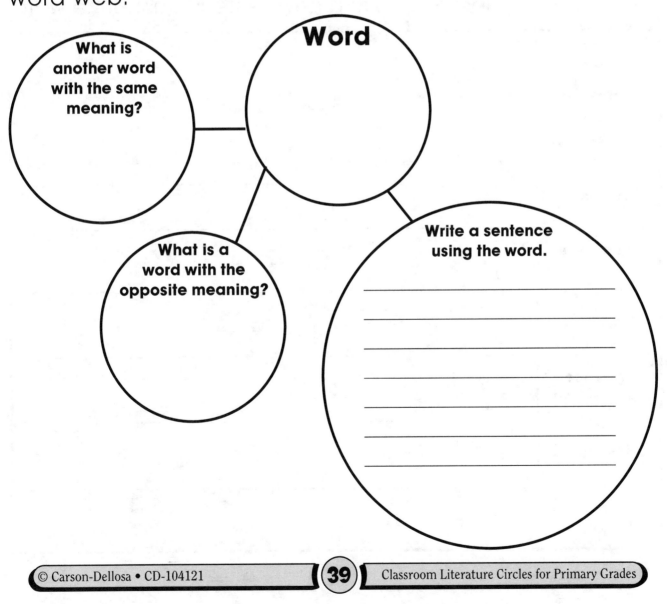

What is another word with the same meaning?

Word

What is a word with the opposite meaning?

Write a sentence using the word.

Name _____

Date _____

Title of Story _____

Read or listen to the story. Choose two words to copy into the word chart. Write a word in the first box. In the second box, copy its sentence from the story. In the third box, write the definition. In the last box, write a new sentence using the word.

Word	
Sentence from the Story	
Definition	
Your Own Sentence	
Word	
Sentence from the Story	
Definition	
Your Own Sentence	

Name _____

Date _____

◯◯◯◯◯◯◯◯◯◯◯◯◯

Title of Story _____

Your job is to make a connection, or "build a bridge," between the story and yourself. Read or listen to the story. Draw a picture in the box that shows how the story reminded you of your own life. Use the lines below the box to write about your picture.

The story reminded me of _____

_____

_____

_____

Name _____

Date _____

◯ ◯ ◯ ◯ ◯ ◯ ◯ ◯ ◯ ◯ ◯ ◯

Title of Story _____

Your job is to make a connection, or "build a bridge," between the story and yourself. Read or listen to the story. Fill in the blanks below. Draw a picture of each sentence in the box.

The character _____ reminds me of _____ because _____ _____ _____ _____	
I know how the character felt when _____ _____ because _____ _____ _____	
The part when _____ _____ reminds me of _____ _____ _____ _____	

Name _____

Date _____

⬤ ⬤ ⬤ ⬤ ⬤ ⬤ ⬤ ⬤ ⬤ ⬤ ⬤ ⬤

Title of Story _____

Your job is to make a connection, or "build a bridge," between the story and yourself. Read or listen to the story. Does a character remind you of someone? Does the story remind you of something that happened to you? Write about the connection between the story and your life. Draw a picture of your writing in the box.

_____

_____

_____

_____

_____

_____

_____

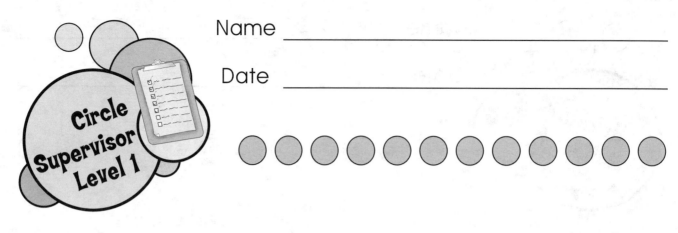

Circle Supervisor Level 1

Your job is to make sure your group works cooperatively and follows directions. You will be the teacher when the teacher is not around. Here are words and phrases to help you do your job. Share them with your group.

Use quiet voices.

Take turns.

Be kind to each other.

Talk about the story.

Share your forms.

Listen.

Look at each other when you speak.

Do your best!

Name _____

Date _____

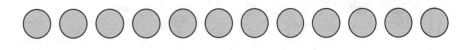

Your job is to guide the group during literature circle time. You will be the teacher when your teacher is not around. You will make sure that everyone is taking turns, following directions, and talking to the group. This form gives you tips to do your job well!

1. Make sure that everyone has time to share.	2. Stay on task.
When group members take too long to finish, you can say: • "We need to move along." • "Let's talk about what the Bridge Builder has to say." • "Let's talk about this later so that everyone has time to share."	If your group starts talking about something other than the story, get them back on track. You can say: • "Okay, everyone, let's get back on track." • "We are off task. Let's get back to work." • "Let's talk about the story. We can talk about this stuff later."
3. Remember that everyone in the circle should share.	4. Use positive language at all times.
If a group member is talking more than everyone else, you can say: • "Abby, you have great ideas today, but let's hear from . . ." If you notice a group member is not sharing, you can say: • "You have been quiet, Ben. We want to know what you think."	Here are some phrases you can use: • "Nice job!" • "Good thinking!" • "Great answer." • "I hadn't thought of it that way. Maybe you're right." • "Great try, but I was thinking . . ." • "Wow, I can tell that was hard for you. Good job!"

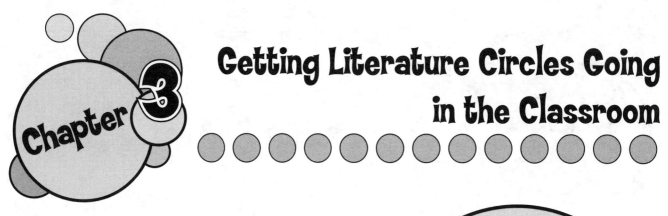

Getting Literature Circles Going in the Classroom

Literature circles can seem complicated and intimidating. Implementing them requires planning, modeling, and organizing. This chapter covers all aspects of start-up, including classroom management and an orderly implementation of each step, to help you get literature circles going in a manageable and realistic way. Once the program is underway, students are in charge, and you are the facilitator. You will quickly realize how easy and worthwhile the process is.

This Chapter Includes:
- a discussion about selecting and obtaining books
- instructions for selecting and rotating groups
- teaching students how to function in groups
- advice about student participation and assessment

Introducing the Concept to Students

First, talk about how literature circles work. If you teach very young, emerging readers, be very general so that you do not confuse or overwhelm them. Simply tell them that they will be starting something called literature circles. At this point, discuss what the word "literature" means and why the process is called a circle. Briefly explain that students will read or listen to a story, and they will have jobs related to the story. Tell them that they will get to share these jobs in groups. If you teach more developed readers or older students, be more specific. Briefly explain the roles and role forms, the schedule (even if you can only estimate it), the means of assessment, and most importantly, the books and book selection process. Once students understand that they will get to talk to each other, they become excited and ready to learn.

Selecting and Obtaining Books

After introducing the concept of literature circles, the next step is to decide whether you or students will choose the literature. Because there can be such a disparity between primary level students, the most important factors in this decision are students' ages and reading abilities. If you teach very young students or emerging readers, or if you feel that implementing literature circles will be challenging enough on its own, select the literature yourself. In this way, you will eliminate the logistical problems that can arise when students select the books and you can take advantage of books that are easy to provide.

As students develop as readers and become familiar with the process, consider letting them choose their own books. This gives students a sense of ownership and they become invested in the activity because they have a stake in making the books "work." Provide a number of related or themed "text sets" and allow students to select the book or books they want to read. For example, have students choose from a bear-themed text set consisting of *Brown Bear, Brown Bear, What Do You See?* by Bill Martin, Jr. (Henry Holt & Co., 1992), *Polar Bear, Polar Bear, What Do You Hear?* by Bill Martin, Jr. (Henry Holt & Co., 1991), *A Pocket for Corduroy* by Don Freeman (Puffin, 1980), and a version of *Goldilocks and the Three Bears*. (See page 61 for suggested themes.) Consider having each student list her choices on a piece of paper in order from most to least desired. If students are able, have them write notes about why they prefer those particular books. Note that if students select nonfiction, many of the forms will not work since they require narrative story elements (such as problem, characters, etc.). Collect the papers and use them to help sort students into groups based on the books they most want to read.

Choosing the Literature
Much of the criteria you will use to select books will depend on your school's curriculum and on students' needs and abilities. Follow these guidelines when choosing books for literature circle groups. The guidelines will be helpful whether you are reading aloud to students or they are reading on their own.

First, the books should be "quality, authentic literature." Literature circle groups are not the venue for responding to basal-type reading materials, such as "consumables," worksheets, activity kits, etc. Such materials tend to be contrived and, because they are prepared for specific academic purposes, often lack the substance of "real literature." If the text is authentic, then students' experiences will be authentic, as well.

Second, although books can be from almost any genre, stick to narratives so that most of the role forms will be useful. Some forms require traditional story elements (characters, problem, solution), and many books do not fulfill this requirement, especially early reader books (such as some by Dr. Seuss or alphabet books). For example, if you selected *Hop on Pop* by Dr. Seuss (Random House, 1963), the My Favorite Part form would work, but the Story Summarizer form would not because there isn't a substantial plot for students to summarize.

Third, the literature must be appropriate for the general reading level of the class. Therefore, select literature that is generally appropriate for your grade level. Chapter 4 (page 70) explains how literature circles help both struggling readers and more proficient readers.

Finally, if you decide to use the same book for the whole class but you do not plan to read the book aloud, then you must acquire a class set of the book. Don't panic! See page 48, which list ways to obtain books. It is ideal for every student to have a copy of the book while completing the literature circle forms and sharing in his group. However, if there are not enough copies for the entire class, make sure students are very familiar with the book through many rereadings. This is especially effective in kindergarten and first grade classrooms, where rereadings are recommended.

If, for whatever reason, you choose not to use the same book for the whole class, each literature circle group can read a different book, and you will need fewer copies of each title. Using more than one title simultaneously allows groups to take turns reading different books and compare or contrast them during whole-class discussions. Consider choosing books with the same author, theme, or genre so that all of the books are connected in some way. Also, having an overall theme provides opportunities to create activities outside of literature circles to supplement students' reading. For example, if using a pet-themed text set, consider creating a supplemental unit around pets in another curriculum area (such as science or art) to coordinate with the theme. (See page 61 for suggested themes.)

Inform students about their book choices by giving a "book talk" (a brief description of each book). Then, as previously described, have students list their preferences in order on sheets of paper. If you assign books to specific groups, reveal the assignments. During this process, you should convey genuine excitement about the selected book or books, especially if you assign them.

Acquiring Book Sets

Again, it is ideal for every student to have a copy of the literature circle book, even if you are reading aloud and students are only using copies for independent role form completion and literature circle discussion. If providing individual copies is not possible, reading aloud from one copy will work fine in primary classrooms because emerging readers will listen to you read and will not read independently. Additionally, since primary teachers commonly reread a story several times throughout the course of a week, students are often familiar enough with the current story to complete their forms and circle discussions without referring directly to the book. On the other hand, if each group reads a different book, acquire a copy for every group member because reading aloud several stories from different groups may confuse young readers and take up too much time.

In either case, plan to acquire classroom sets of some titles. Regardless of how many copies you need, there are many ways to increase the size of your classroom library.
- Scout the school library for multiple copies of books.
- Find colleagues who are "book collectors" and will lend books.
- Search local bookstores—especially larger franchises—because they usually offer discounts to teachers. Some even provide membership cards that offer discounts.
- Shop at used bookstores—they can be gold mines for educators!
- Browse garage sales and flea markets for children's books.
- Join a school book club. They are excellent sources for purchasing books at discount prices, and they often offer free books as incentives for teachers.
- Apply for grants. Although challenging to win, a grant is an excellent way to acquire funds for books.
- Use the Donation Letter (page 63) to request donations from parents. Alter it slightly for businesses, bookstores, etc.
- Finally, ask parents to help if it is appropriate for the school population. Once parents understand the need for these books, they are often happy to contribute. Use the Donation Letter (page 63) or a parents' night to explain the reading program and the benefits of using authentic literature. Provide parents with a book wish list or incorporate your request into a school fund-raiser.

Selecting and Rotating Groups

Deciding What Factors Will Determine Group Selection
Each "circle" is considered a group. There are many ways to select group members. Remember that each circle must be small (four to five students) and efficient.

If students select books and form groups accordingly, the number of students interested in a particular title will determine group size. If you choose this method of group selection but anticipate having more requests for a book than you have copies available, have students list a few books in order of preference so that you can try to give everyone his first or second choice.

If groups are not based on literature selection, there are several decisions to make about how to form groups. Sometimes you will need to choose who will work with whom, based on several factors. First, there is the question of using heterogeneous groups (students with mixed abilities) versus homogeneous groups (students with similar abilities). Heterogeneous grouping can be very effective in literature circles because more proficient readers can support struggling ones. However, homogeneous grouping may better meet the needs of some students. Second, you may want to pair particular students or keep others apart for personality reasons. Third, you may want to assign students to groups based on the reading levels of books you are using, giving easy books to less proficient students. Finally, remember that every class is different—some years, students just seem to work well together. In other years, regardless of great effort on your part, student-selected groups lead to conflict. Use trial and error; experiment with different selection methods and adjust as necessary.

After students have been participating in literature circles effectively for some time, they may be ready to choose their own groups because they know what is expected of them. Allowing students to form their own groups, as long as they show they can do it in an effective manner, can serve as a reward for successful group work.

Planning a System for Group Rotation
Most teachers who use literature circles recommend having the groups remain the same throughout the course of a book (unless, of course, the group members are not working well together). Working with the same group members helps students develop a rapport with each other, meaning that as students work together throughout the duration of a book, they will often develop their own dialogue. Additionally, group members can refer back to a discussion that occurred during a previous meeting or make connections between one chapter and another. But, after the first book is complete, don't let things get too comfortable. Create new groups with each new book so that students can work with new classmates. Introducing new combinations of students keeps the process fresh and interesting, and if there is tension between group members, they can easily be separated. You will also have the opportunity to match students to groups with students who have complementary skills. For example, you can pair a strong reader with a weaker one or a student who is good at asking questions and soliciting answers with a student who is reluctant to speak.

Note that rotating groups each time a new book is started may only apply to older students who are using beginning chapter books and novels which cannot be completed in one reading. Since picture books are often completed in one reading, group rotation may need to be determined by other factors, unless you prefer that students' groups change frequently. If you prefer to keep groups constant for a certain period of time, then rotate groups every month or few weeks or each time you begin a new theme.

Teaching Students How to "Do" Literature Circles

Explaining and Modeling Role Forms
After having the general discussion about literature circles, start training students how to complete each step. Beginning with the reproducible role forms in Chapter 2, which cover key story elements as well as beginning reading skills. Choose from the variety of forms and formats in order to best suit students' abilities.

Modeling and teaching one role at a time, especially at the beginning and with younger students, helps clarify the requirements for each role. First, decide if you will select from the Level 1–Basic role forms or Level 2–Traditional role forms. Refer to Chapter 2 for details about the two different types.

Next, decide whether each student in a group will use the same role form or different forms. If you are working with very young children or if you prefer to simplify the initial teaching stage, you may want to use only one role form for the entire class. In this way, students will only be required to learn one role and how to share it in their groups; they won't be overwhelmed with too many role forms or by what is expected during group time. Also, note that young students may feel more comfortable if you first allow groups to take turns simulating literature circles within the whole-class setting. Then, when you introduce the actual book students will use, they will have already participated in the group process.

Once students understand the literature circle concept and know what is expected of them, you can teach new role forms so that eventually everyone in the group completes and shares a different form each time. Whether you plan to teach students how to complete several role forms or use one role for the whole class, the best way to do it is through modeling. Begin by reading a selection from a familiar book. Make a transparency of the role form and place it on an overhead projector. (Some teachers prefer to model this role form on the board or even in small groups, depending on what they feel is the best format for their students.) Model the completion of the form by thinking aloud and explaining each step as you complete it on the transparency. Then, read another familiar selection and guide students as they complete their own forms. Review their work and make adjustments or reteach if necessary.

If you are only teaching one role form, stop here. If you are teaching students how to complete more role forms, repeat the process introducing one role form each day one until students know how to complete all of the role forms. The total number of role forms you choose to teach (and then use) will depend in part on how quickly students pick up the process. For example, if you have four students in each literature circle, you might choose to teach four different role forms. If students learn the process quickly, you can then add or substitute new forms. For example, if students started literature circles with four forms from Level 1–Basic (such as My Favorite Part, Liked/Did Not Like, New Book Cover, and I Want to Share), after a few weeks, you might decide to teach My Opinion and Book Review and substitute these new roles for two of the others.

Allotting Time for Group Meetings
As you set up time expectations for literature circles, do what works best for students and the class routine. There is no set time frame, but if you are working with younger, emerging readers, the time will be significantly shorter than if students are more advanced. Following are some general guidelines.

If you are working with young students and emerging readers, allot:
- 25 minutes for reading and role form completion (even if you read aloud to students),
- 10 minutes for circle discussions, and
- 5 minutes for whole-class discussion.

If you are working with students who are older and more advanced, allot:
- 35 minutes for reading and role form completion,
- 20 minutes for circle discussions, and
- 10 minutes for whole-class discussion.

The time allotment for each part of the process is another aspect of literature circles that is dictated by your needs and preferences. If only a limited amount of time is available, shorten the allotted class time for reading the assignment and ask students to read more for homework. They can then be ready to complete the role forms during one class session and meet to discuss in their circles on the following day. Another option might be to divide the literature circle steps into two days: read and complete role forms one day and have circle discussions and whole-class discussion the next.

On the other hand, students may be so involved in their circles on a particular day that you let them continue their discussions. It is important to note, however, that the reading portion (especially if it is independent, silent reading) should not be too lengthy. If the reading assignment is too long, some students may be overwhelmed, and their comprehension and responses will suffer. Focus on quality, not quantity.

Choosing Group Meeting Spaces
The classroom size and layout, as well as grade level, will largely determine students' group meeting locations. As shown in the scenarios (page 7), many kindergarten teachers (especially early in the year) want to keep students sitting in their groups from the very beginning to avoid movement, distractions, and confusion. Older students can usually handle working independently at their seats and then meeting group members at a predetermined location.

If you have a large, open classroom, simply assign locations around the room. If there is limited space, be more creative. It is surprising how well students can focus in small groups, even in crowded areas. Use as much of the classroom space as possible, but if necessary, have students meet at their desks or on the floor. Or, try one of these options:

- Divide the room by hanging fabric from clotheslines, making sure you can still see students easily. This designates cozy meeting areas and helps buffer noise. It is also especially helpful for easily distracted young ones!
- Let one or two groups at a time meet quietly during other seat work.
- Use blankets on the floor to designate group meeting spaces. Each group of students stays on their own blanket.
- Push desks into completely new arrangements just for literature circles. This creates a break between group meetings and other schoolwork.
- If centers are set up around the room for other subject area times, use these areas for literature circle groups.
- If a teacher in a nearby classroom has a different lunch schedule, ask to use that space and schedule your literature circle time accordingly.

Another consideration when assigning group meeting spaces is the noise level. With a classroom full of students talking in groups, it will not be quiet. The noise level can take getting used to. It can also pose a problem for surrounding classrooms or for a teacher whose room in is a studio setting. If there are other classes nearby, train students to talk quietly while in their groups. This is also noted on the Level 1 Circle Supervisor's form (page 44.) Turn the lights off and on to alert students when the volume is getting too high. Praise and reward groups who work quietly and efficiently.

An ideal solution for a small or overly noisy classroom is to simply leave it. Prop open the classroom door and have one or two groups meet in the hallway. Reserve a section of the library for "remote" meetings. If weather permits and your room opens to a field or outdoor area, have another group take advantage of that space by meeting outside. Before students leave the classroom, make sure they know the rules for being outside of the room. Consider using this as an incentive for groups who work well together. For safety reasons, make sure students are always supervised by a qualified adult. If you have parent volunteers, teacher's assistants, or even older students from intermediate grade levels, have them "chaperone" groups that are working outside of the classroom. (If you have older students who are chaperoning, make sure an adult is available to check on them frequently.)

Informing Groups about Where to Meet
To avoid confusion or conflict, mark the various group meeting areas with colorful tape; affix small signs to the floor, walls, or clotheslines; or display a small classroom map with the group locations. You may also post copies of the different book covers or let students design signs that depict themes, characters, or events in the books. Create signs that are more graphic and illustrative for younger students.

Organizing Supplies, Groups, and Role Forms

In order for literature circles to run efficiently, students must know at a glance where supplies are kept, what groups they are in, and which roles they are completing. Especially if the whole class is reading the same book, students may have trouble keeping even their groups in mind at first. Fortunately, few supplies are required to organize for literature circles. You need only to organize the book sets, role forms, and any materials students need to understand what their roles are and where their groups meet.

For very young students distribute the role forms each time students will participate in literature circles. This may take more time at the beginning of each session. However, it could take even more time if students try to organize themselves at the start of each session and need your help to get into groups, find the appropriate forms, etc.

For students who are old enough to be more autonomous, one easy option is to store books and blank role forms in a literature circle center or pocket chart. If students can work somewhat independently, each student will be able to go to the center, take a book, find her assigned role form, and start the day's reading. Even if students are younger or if you are reading the story aloud and guiding the steps, having a literature circle center will help keep the materials handy, organized, and accessible.

Another option for older students is to have them keep track of the role forms and/or the text sets. Students can keep blank copies of the role forms they will be completing in their own role form folders. They can also keep completed role forms that you do not collect in these folders. Once students get comfortable with literature circles, you will only need to remind them of their roles for the day and assign the reading selection. They can then simply take the required forms out of their folders and get to work. The folders are also practical because students have all of their literature circle forms together, making it easy for students to refer back to them to see their growth and improvement. Students also like to keep books at their desks. If a student reads ahead, it will be easier for her to use a bookmark to mark her place in the book if she keeps it at her desk.

After you decide how to organize supplies, focus on organizing students and roles. One way to help young students remember their groups is to create role tags for them to wear. Copy a set of role tags (pages 59–60) on a different-colored paper for each group. Laminate the tags, then punch holes in the tops and cut them apart. Add yarn to create role necklaces. (You can also use different colors of yarn for each group to differentiate the tags.) To change roles, simply have students exchange necklaces. To change groups, have students choose new tags, then group students by the tags' colors. This method takes more time in the beginning because you have to make the necklaces, but it makes group organization visual and more concrete for younger students. To give students more ownership of the process, let them make and decorate a class set of role tags. Then, let students designate a special place in the classroom to store them. Each time older students change books, consider letting them decorate a new set of role tags in a theme similar to each book or series of books they will be reading. (This last method will be too time-consuming if students are reading or listening to very short books.)

A simple, effective way to help more independent students stay organized is to post a literature circle chart on a bulletin board, a laminated piece of poster board, or a pocket chart. For the Level 2 roles, write students' names on index cards and copy the role tags (pages 59–60). Organize each group horizontally on one line. (Use thumbtacks or hook-and-loop tape to attach cards and tags to the bulletin board or poster board.) Each time students participate in literature circles, rotate either students' name cards or the role tags. Do this before each literature circle session so that students know their roles.

Keeping track of the Circle Supervisor is similar to keeping track of other roles. Some teachers like to designate that students who have particular roles always serve as the Circle Supervisors. For example, you may decide that students who are serving as Imaginative Illustrators will always be the Circle Supervisors as well. Another way to indicate the Circle Supervisors for the day is to make colorful tags, then rotate the tags on the literature circle chart. If you are using the role tag necklaces, have each Circle Supervisor wear two necklaces or attach a colorful clothespin to his role necklace.

Regardless of how you choose to organize the groups, it is critical to rotate roles regularly so that each student gets a chance to serve as a Circle Supervisor and practice the reading strategies on each form. Rotating roles and groups also helps keep the process fresh and interesting for students.

Modeling Literature Circle Action for Students
When the preparation and the classroom management decisions are finalized, it is time to teach students what to do in the circles. Be warned: no matter how many times or ways you go over the process, students will likely need some redirection. You can be clear with all directions, explanations, and expectations, and still encounter some problems the first few times you actually do literature circles, especially with very young students. Following a few reteaching sessions, both you and students will adapt, and literature circles will run smoothly.

After students learn to complete the role forms based on the day's literature, they must learn what is expected when they are in their groups. Remind them that literature circles are groups of students who are reading the same book and gathering to discuss what they read. You want students to read or be read to, complete the role forms, and then gather in their groups to talk, share, and debate. Role forms are guides for the discussions and will serve as catalysts for debates (especially with older, more proficient students). Explain that when groups meet, students should take turns sharing their role form responses and exploring each other's thoughts. Of course, your expectations (and thus what you teach students at this step) will depend greatly on students' ages and reading abilities.

For kindergartners, the process for the circle is similar to, but more simplistic than, the process used with older students. See the following examples (page 55).

Aidan, a kindergartner, has completed the My Favorite Part role form (from Level 1–Basic). He will first share his role form responses, then turn to his group members and ask them to also share their favorite parts (even if they completed different forms). After all group members have shared, it is the next member's turn. Beth shares her completed I Want to Share role form, then asks each member to verbally share some aspect of the story or comment on and ask questions about her form. This process continues until all of the group members have shared their roles and discussed them with the other group members.

Note that if you are working with very young, emerging readers, you might have chosen to use the same role form for everyone in the group. In that case, the process would still be the same except that each member would share the same form and the discussion would consist of sharing, comparing, and contrasting the completed role forms.

With older students, the group process is more interactive. For example, Casey is a second grader who is serving as Circle Supervisor for the day. In his group, he turns to Abigail, who has the Story Summarizer role (from Level 2–Traditional), and tells her to go first. She will first share her role form responses and then turn to her group members and ask each, in turn, what he would add. Throughout this process, Casey is directing—making sure each student responds to Abigail, each student has taken a turn, etc. Then, Casey calls on Benjamin, who is the Question Creator. It is now Benjamin's turn to share his role form responses. He asks his first question and invites each group member, in turn, to offer her answer (preferably as they all refer to their copies of the book). After all group members have answered, Benjamin shares his answer, and the group discusses, debates, and comments. This process continues until all group members have shared and discussed their roles. Remember, the entire process is "supervised" by the Circle Supervisor, but as students get more comfortable, the Circle Supervisor's job should become almost nonexistent because students want to participate and know what is expected. After students have learned the process, the Circle Supervisor only redirects fellow group members or turns to you for assistance, as necessary, when you are not nearby.

Whether you are working with students who belong in one of the two examples above or somewhere in between, the best way for them to understand what is expected in a literature circle is to briefly explain and then role-play a group meeting. Select a group of students to demonstrate for the whole class what a literature circle looks and sounds like. As the rest of the class looks on, participate in a literature circle and redirect students in your "group" if necessary. Another way to model the literature circle discussions and involve more students in the role-playing is to do a "class circle." This way, all students can be active and participate rather than just watch and listen. However, due to the size of this circle, the discussions will be very superficial. Depending on how much time you have allotted for this instruction and role-playing session, you may then choose to proceed with the actual first literature circle meetings or repeat the role-playing and wait to begin the circles another day.

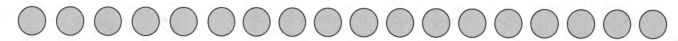

Defining the Teacher's Role

Deciding Where to Be During Group Work

When introducing literature circles, especially to young children, it is often effective to run one circle as a whole class so that all students are involved and can learn what is expected. Although large groups are not effective literature circles, this strategy can be helpful early on just to simulate a discussion and demonstrate how a group discussion should run. During the whole-class phase, your presence as teacher and leader is critical—you will serve as the Circle Supervisor for the entire group (class) as you model the process and redirect students as needed.

As teachers, we often hear buzz words such as *facilitator* and *guide*. Unfortunately, curriculum requirements and student needs do not always allow teachers to fill these roles. Literature circles provide the ideal environment for you to serve as both facilitator and guide. Exactly what you do during each session will depend on students' ages and how long the class has been participating in literature circles. If students are very young or are just learning the process, then you will be observing, guiding, redirecting, and modeling. After holding literature circles in a whole class setting or if students are older or have been doing literature circles for a while, you will still observe and occasionally redirect as students participate, but your role will be mainly that of facilitator.

If students are reading independently, read silently with students to act as a model while participating in the day's activities. If students are still too young to read independently, then read aloud to the class or groups. As students work on their role forms, circulate around the room to assist and encourage on-task behavior. It is especially critical that you provide guidance during role form completion for students who are still emerging as readers and writers. These younger students will also need for you to keep track of the time for reading, role form completion, and group discussion. Older and more independent students who have finished their role forms may need to be reminded to go to their meeting locations to wait for the rest of their group members. Be sure to observe these "early birds" to ensure that they are rereading the selections, reviewing their work, or doing another related activity. (See pages 73–74 for more ideas for these students.)

After students have joined their groups, you can participate in the circle discussions in a number of ways. At first, you will want to spend some time with each group in order to observe and assess their interaction. How much time you spend with each group may depend on how involved you get in a particular circle, how much redirection a group needs, and/or how much time is allotted for literature circles on that day. When first entering a group, it is a good idea just to sit and observe so that students realize that they are responsible for the work of leading and participating. However, if the discussion comes to a halt, you may want to prompt students to continue the discussion.

Very young students will need more guidance and assistance during literature circle time. Be as available as possible to all groups at the beginning. Consider enlisting volunteers to sit in on groups and assist younger students as they experiment and develop during their literature circle discussions. Volunteers can be parents, community helpers, teacher's assistants, or even older students from the school. Also consider implementing literature circles with a colleague who teaches a higher grade level and ask for volunteers from among her students.

Once students get used to the idea that you will occasionally join a group, they will not be intimidated by your presence. Most of the time, elementary students (especially the primary level ones!) actually want their teachers to join them and will be especially eager and motivated. After students are comfortable, you may choose to participate with one group during the whole session and then switch groups next time. Keep in mind, however, that in order for this to be effective, the other groups must be capable of running smoothly, independently, and efficiently, since you will not be circulating. You may opt to record an audiotape of one or more groups when you are not available to work with everyone, particularly if you prefer to participate in one group per session. This will help keep students on track and will also help you monitor their progress at your leisure.

Monitoring "Nonteacher" Groups
The nature of literature circles in a well-run classroom is intrinsically motivating. Therefore, students should participate, discuss, and "do what they're supposed to do" without much redirection. If, at first, the process does not work as smoothly as it should, the Circle Supervisors must remind members to "get back on task." Remember that they serve as the groups' teachers when you are not nearby. Students should recall how to act as Circle Supervisors from the modeling sessions, so they will know how to use positive language to keep the groups focused. But, circulate to diminish the possibility of off-task behaviors. If there are problems, refer to Chapter 4 for more information.

Another way to inspire groups to do well even when you are not present is to have students occasionally fill out assessment worksheets (pages 64–67). There are four types of these worksheets. The Self-Assessment worksheets (page 64–65) give each student an opportunity to think about and evaluate his work and effort during circle time. The Group Assessment worksheets (pages 66–67) give each student an opportunity to evaluate his fellow group members' work and efforts.

Finally, the best motivator is the Circle Star worksheets (pages 68–69). Each student in the group should fill out a Circle Star worksheet, nominating one student as the "star" of the group. There are several ways to use this form. First, it can serve as a progress report. Hopefully each student will be chosen as a Circle Star at some point, but if not, plan to observe those particular students and their groups more carefully. A second use is to help you decide, as students near the end of a book, how to create new groups for the next round of literature circles. You can evenly disperse your "stars" into new groups after they are identified, or put them all in one group to give other students a chance to shine. A third way to use the Circle Star worksheets is to periodically ask students if any group members did such an outstanding job that they deserve to be nominated as Circle Stars for the day. These Circle Stars can be displayed on a "Wall of Fame" bulletin board in the room to keep students motivated to

do their best work in order to be recognized by peers. A final way is to assign each group member a different student to write about on a Circle Star worksheet so that each student reads positive feedback about herself. Regardless of how you use the Circle Star worksheets, be sure to model how to recognize commendable effort and write positive feedback.

The Whole-Group Wrap-Up

The last part of the actual literature circles activity is the whole-class discussion. After students have completed the reading, filled out the role forms, met in their groups, shared their roles, and discussed the day's reading, they should return to the whole-group setting. Whole-group time can last from two to as long as 10 minutes. Use this time to fulfill several objectives:
- serve as a review of the day's reading
- give closure to the lesson and activities
- clear up confusion or answer questions that arose during the circles
- address logistical problems (noise level, too much movement around the room, etc.)
- allow groups time to share how their meetings went and talk about what part of the reading on which they focused
- provide students with encouragement and feedback so that they can be more on track next time
- pass out and complete any assessment or Circle Star worksheets

Use the wrap-up time for any purpose that is appropriate for your class. Each wrap-up may be different because of students' needs, and it is a good idea to let students direct some of the conversation. Let them share what they learned and what they did well. Ask open and broad questions when the class comes back together. This will lead to more discussions, rather than seem like "quiz time." Praise students when possible and jot down notes about how the sessions seemed to go. If any groups seem to have little to say or limit their comments to negative or nonspecific remarks, plan to sit in on those groups during the next literature circle session.

Time to Celebrate!

You did it! Your students will continue to improve their literature circle skills with each session. Reward the class for doing a good job or consider a book-themed celebration when the first books are finished. Consider doing one of the following types of celebrations:
- Allow students to dress as their favorite characters from the books they have read.
- Serve food mentioned in one of the books. (When planning a food activity, be sure to get families' permission and check for food allergies and religious and other food preferences.)
- Let students redraw artwork from the role forms and post them in an in-class art gallery. Allow students to design parent invitations to the class art show.
- If the completed books are short and students are capable, let students act them out as you read.

Using the Assessment Worksheets

In addition to using assessment worksheets to evaluate students' performances during literature circles, you can use these worksheets to manage the groups. The assessment worksheets also provide students with a safe method to voice any concerns, confusion, or complaints that they may be reluctant to verbalize. When evaluating students' completed assessment forms, note any patterns that point to existing or potential problems. For example, you may notice that a particular group's members are complaining about one student's lack of participation. Or, one student's self-assessment could indicate that he does not feel he is doing well in literature circles. Perhaps one student is chosen as the Circle Star repeatedly, which could mean she is doing much more work than the rest of her group members. Use these or other clues to help you choose which groups to visit and how to form the next round of groups.

Choose from the six assessment worksheets (pages 64–69) depending on students' needs and your objectives. Consider using a different assessment each time so that sometimes students are evaluating themselves, their group members, or both. Some students do not handle group evaluations well (are not honest, use them to praise only their friends, etc.) and may benefit most from self-assessment worksheets. Others, especially younger students, may not do well with self-assessment worksheets. The Circle Star worksheet may be used for every literature circle discussion or perhaps sporadically so that it remains a "big deal." One way to motivate students to want to do well enough to be nominated as Circle Stars is to display the worksheets on a bulletin board or send them home to families.

Role Tags

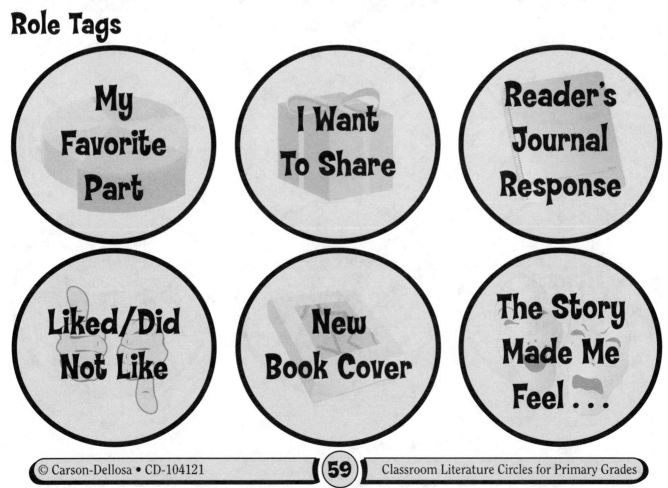

Role Tags (continued)

Book Review

My Opinion

Story Summarizer

Question Creator

Imaginative Illustrator

Word Watcher

Bridge Builder

Circle Supervisor Level 1

Circle Supervisor Level 2

Book and Theme Suggestions

This list highlights books that can be grouped into themes for literature circles. Read all books yourself before sharing them with students. A few of these books may be above some students' independent reading levels, but sharing them aloud several times will allow all students to react to the literature. Also, note that there are usually many editions available of most titles, and not all copies need to be the same.

Text Set Themes

Anger, Bad Moods, Irritability, Tantrums

Alexander and the Terrible, Horrible, No Good, Very Bad Day by Judith Viorst (Aladdin, 1987)

Andrew's Angry Words by Dorothea Lachner (North-South Books, 1997)

Bel and Bub and the Bad Snowball by Jan Pieńkowski (Penguin, 2000)

Don't Let the Pigeon Drive the Bus! by Mo Willems (Hyperion, 2003)

Elbert's Bad Word by Audrey Wood (Voyager, 1996)

Goldie Is Mad by Margie Palatini (Hyperion, 2001)

The Grouchy Ladybug by Eric Carle (HarperCollins, 1996)

Lila Bloom by Alexander Stadler (Farrar, Straus and Giroux, 2004)

Lilly's Purple Plastic Purse by Kevin Henkes (Greenwillow, 1996)

No, David! by David Shannon (Blue Sky Press, 1998)

When Sophie Gets Angry—Really, Really Angry . . . by Molly Bang (Blue Sky Press, 1999)

Where the Wild Things Are by Maurice Sendak (HarperCollins, 1988)

Families

Abuela by Arthur Dorros (Puffin, 1997)

Amelia Bedelia's Family Album by Peggy Parish (HarperTrophy, 2003)

If I Ran the Family by Lee and Sue Kaiser Johnson (Free Spirit, 1992)

Love You Forever by Robert Munsch (Firefly Books, 1986)

My Rotten Redheaded Older Brother by Patricia Polacco (Aladdin, 1998)

Ramona Quimby, Age 8 by Beverly Cleary (HarperTrophy, 1992)

The Relatives Came by Cynthia Rylant (Aladdin, 1993)

Sarah, Plain and Tall by Patricia MacLachlan (HarperTrophy, 1987)

The Table Where Rich People Sit by Byrd Baylor (Aladdin, 1998)

Feeling Left Out

Coat of Many Colors by Dolly Parton (HarperTrophy, 1996)

The Chalk Box Kid by Clyde Robert Bulla (Random House, 1987)

Chrysanthemum by Kevin Henkes (HarperTrophy, 1996)

Freckle Juice by Judy Blume (Yearling, 1978)

I'm Not Invited? by Diana Cain Bluthenthal (Atheneum, 2003)

King of the Playground by Phyllis Reynolds Naylor (Aladdin, 1994)

Leo the Late Bloomer by Robert Kraus (HarperTrophy, 1994)

Recess Queen by Alexis O'Neill (Scholastic, 2002)

Stellaluna by Janell Cannon (Harcourt, 1993)

Tacky the Penguin by Helen Lester (Houghton Mifflin, 1990)

Thank You, Mr. Falker by Patricia Polacco (Philomel, 1998)

Friendship

Best Friends by Steven Kellogg (Dial, 1986)

Frog and Toad Together by Arnold Lobel (HarperTrophy, 1979)

The Giving Tree by Shel Silverstein (HarperCollins, 1964)

Ira Sleeps Over by Bernard Waber (Houghton Mifflin, 1975)

Mitchell Is Moving by Marjorie Weinman Sharmat (Aladdin, 1996)

Problem Solving

Are You My Mother? by P. D. Eastman (Random House, 1960)

Click, Clack, Moo: Cows That Type by Doreen Cronin (Simon & Schuster, 2000)

Elbert's Bad Word by Audrey Wood (Voyager, 1996)

Lilly's Purple Plastic Purse by Kevin Henkes (Greenwillow, 1996)

One of Each by Mary Ann Hoberman (Megan Tingley, 2000)

School

First Day Jitters by Julie Danneberg (Charlesbridge, 2000)

Junie B., First Grader (At Last!) by Barbara Park (Random House, 2002)

Lilly's Purple Plastic Purse by Kevin Henkes (Greenwillow, 1996)

Miss Bindergarten Gets Ready for Kindergarten by Joseph Slate (Puffin, 2001)

Miss Nelson Is Missing! by Harry Allard (Houghton Mifflin, 1985)

Thank You, Mr. Falker by Patricia Polacco (Philomel, 1998)

Dear Families,

Research shows that quality literature should be the core of any good reading program. Therefore, we will be using children's books as part of our classroom reading curriculum. One of our most exciting literature-based activities will be literature circles. Literature circles are "circles" (groups) of approximately five students that gather on a regular basis to discuss the books they are reading in class. The purpose of literature circles is to get students to think about, discuss, and even debate quality literature.

Of course, when children's literature is the foundation of a reading program, students must have many books. Ideally, there should be enough copies of the same book for each child to have his or her own copy for the duration of the book activities (a class set). Other times, enough copies of one book for a small group of students to use (a text set) will suffice.

We have already acquired many copies of various books, but we are always in need of more. If you would like to donate any children's books to our classroom collection, it would be greatly appreciated. Here are two ways that you can make a donation.

- Donate books your family has already read.
- Purchase one copy, one text set (____ books), or even a class set (____ books) for the class at a local bookstore, used bookstore, or other vendor.

Although any book donation is a great help, below is a list of priority or preferred books we need. Please let me know if you have any questions or comments. Thank you very much for your support and assistance.

Book Title	Author	Publication Information	Number of Books Needed

Sincerely,

_____

Self-Assessment Level 1

Title of Story _____

Group Members _____

Use this worksheet to review how you did during literature circles. Circle the smiley face if you agree with the sentence. Circle the sad face if you do not agree with the sentence. Be honest!

	Agree	**Disagree**
1. I finished today's reading on time.	☺	☹
2. I did my best work on my role form.	☺	☹
3. I talked about my role form with my group.	☺	☹
4. I was a good listener.	☺	☹
5. I was nice to my group members.	☺	☹
6. I did my very best.	☺	☹

Self-Assessment Level 2

Name _____

Date _____

Title of Story _____

Group Members _____

Use this worksheet to review how you and your group did during literature circles. Circle YES or NO to show if you agree with each sentence. You may write comments on the lines at the bottom of the page. Be honest!

1. I finished the day's reading on time.   YES   NO

2. I finished my role form to the best of my ability.   YES   NO

3. I talked about my role form with my group.   YES   NO

4. I was a good listener.   YES   NO

5. I used positive language when I talked.   YES   NO

6. I did my very best.   YES   NO

_____

_____

_____

Name _____

Date _____

Group Assessment Level 1

○○○○○○○○○○○○

Title of Story _____

Group Members _____

Use this worksheet to review how you and your group did during literature circles. Circle the smiley face if you agree with the sentence. Circle the sad face if you do not agree with the sentence. Write each group member's name under one category at the bottom of the page.

	Agree	**Disagree**
1. My group worked well together.	☺	☺
2. My group members completed the role forms.	☺	☺
3. My group shared and talked about the role forms.	☺	☺
4. My group members were good listeners.	☺	☺
5. My group members were nice to each other.	☺	☺

Worked Hard	**Needed to Help More**
_____	_____
_____	_____
_____	_____
_____	_____

Name _____

Date _____

Group Assessment Level 2

Title of Story _____

Group Members _____

Use this worksheet to review how you and your group did during literature circles. Circle yes or no for each sentence. Then, explain your answer.

1. My group worked well together.   YES   NO

    _____

    _____

2. My group members finished the role forms to the best of
    their abilities.   YES   NO

    _____

    _____

3. My group shared and talked about the role forms.   YES   NO

    _____

    _____

4. My group members were good listeners.   YES   NO

    _____

    _____

5. My group members used positive language when
    we talked.   YES   NO

    _____

    _____

Circle Star Level 1

Name _____

Date _____

Title of Story _____

Group Members _____

Name a group member who you feel did a great job during literature circle time. Draw a picture of the Circle Star below.

_____ should be the Circle Star because _____

_____

_____

Name _____

Date _____

Circle Star Level 2

◯ ◯ ◯ ◯ ◯ ◯ ◯ ◯ ◯ ◯ ◯ ◯

Title of Story _____

Group Members _____

Name a group member who you feel did a great job during literature circle time.

The Circle Star today is _____

Reasons this student should be the Circle Star: _____

_____

_____

_____

_____

_____

_____

_____

Troubleshooting and FAQs

Now that literature circles are a regular part of your class reading program, some problems, challenges, and "technical difficulties" may arise. This chapter addresses questions and provides possible solutions for some of those obstacles. Literature circles, like most other classroom activities, can usually be adapted to your particular teaching situation. If you come across a problem that is not addressed here, take a step back and look at it as you would any other teaching situation.

This Chapter Includes Answers to Common Questions Addressing:

- working literature circles into a reading program
- adapting literature circles for young students
- reteaching students how to "do" literature circles
- troubleshooting for problem groups and students

How do literature circles fit into my current reading program?

One reason why it is so simple to add literature circles to the regular list of activities in your reading classroom is that you can decide where and when they fit into the current reading program. How literature circles fit in will depend on the current classroom framework and curriculum. Curricular requirements vary from state to state and even school to school. You may have more limitations than other teachers, or you may have the freedom to "plug in" literature circles wherever and whenever you see fit. Determining how and where literature circles will fit in based on school requirements is the first step. For many teachers, books chosen for literature circles are at the core of their reading programs, so the circles blend into their existing reading programs seamlessly. Other teachers build their reading programs around the books they and their students decide to use for literature circles. Consider, for example, a second-grade class that is reading *Freckle Juice* by Judy Blume (Yearling, 1978). On days of the week that students do not participate in literature circles, they would participate in other reading activities also based on *Freckle Juice*, such as holding a writing workshop, having taped read-aloud time, continuing daily phonics lessons, working on vocabulary, etc.

How often should I do literature circles?

The frequency of meetings depends on many factors. One factor to consider is the guidelines of your school's (or district's, state's, or province's) reading program. If you have the power to determine the frequency of literature circles, note that they are not meant to be the sole component of your reading program. You must incorporate other skills, activities, and lessons in order to have an effective reading program. Especially for prereaders, phonological awareness activities may take up the bulk of their reading instruction time. A good rule of thumb at first is to have students meet in circles approximately once a week. As students become familiar with the routine and need less reteaching, you may decide to increase the number of sessions per week because there will not be as much time devoted to reviewing the procedures, and literature circles can be more of a main component.

If your teaching situation restricts your choice of activities, this may mean that you can only hold literature circle meetings every two weeks and not always on consecutive books or chapters. Or, you may be required to base literature activities only on required reading selections. Students will still benefit, however, from the discussion, the variation of roles and activities, and the book club atmosphere that literature circles provide.

I have every range of reading level in my primary class, from emerging readers to more developed and proficient readers. How can I adapt literature circles for all students, regardless of their reading levels?

There are many ways to adapt literature circles to fit every student's needs. Use your professional judgment to decide what is best for students.

- First, begin with Level 1–Basic role forms. These are simple enough to be adaptable for the emerging readers, but a more proficient reader will still benefit from the format and responses.
- Consider having nonreaders complete only the illustrative portions of the role forms, while requiring more developed students to draw and write their responses.
- Use dictation with nonreaders. Have these students dictate what they want to write to you (or a volunteer, such as a parent or older student), as you record it on their forms. They will still be able to share their responses in their groups since they know what they "wrote."
- Pair each struggling student with a classmate so that they can complete the day's role forms together. This "buddy" can be from the struggling student's literature circle group or can be someone from another group who has the same role for the day. (For example, two students completing the My Favorite Part role form can work together on their role forms.) The latter may be the better option because it enables two students to complete the same role but present to different groups.
- Use this opportunity to be the struggling reader's buddy. Helping struggling readers is an excellent opportunity for teacher-student one-on-one. If you have more than one nonreader, consider working with this small group all at the same time. Or, enlist the help of a volunteer.
- Lastly, remember that the setting of literature circles itself will automatically support these emerging readers. When students join for their groups and discuss their roles, the other members will add their ideas and thoughts, so the emerging reader will be assisted by her circle members.

I have a student who is not writing yet and is very hesitant to use invented spelling. How can he complete the role form so that he can still participate?

Emerging and hesitant student writers may need some creative help in completing their forms. This should not deter you from doing literature circles in your classroom! The benefits are tremendous, maybe even more so for these emerging readers and writers. Remember that doing literature circles is a verbal, social activity, so these students will still be able to succeed. If nonwriters are hesitant or afraid to use invented spelling (as so many kindergartners are early in the year), try having them dictate their responses to you, a volunteer, or a more proficient student. Another option might be to have the student record his responses and play the tape at his group meeting. Finally, if these options are not possible, simply have the student use the illustration portions of the role forms until he is ready to try the writing.

I spend the first half of the year just teaching my kindergarten students the letters of the alphabet and how to write their names. Is it realistic to think I can incorporate literature circles into my classroom?

Yes! Even kindergartners can do literature circles when the activity is taken down to its most basic aspects. First, do the reading portion as a read-aloud. Use familiar literature that students have already heard several times. Being familiar with the text will make it easier for them to complete this higher-order activity.

Also, select Level 1–Basic forms and begin by using the same one for the entire class. For example, if you choose to use the My Favorite Part form, everyone in the class should complete this form, and all students will be sharing their favorite parts during literature circle time. Very young students will be learning to share their literature responses with groups of their peers, and inevitably, conversations will ensue (in this case, about which part of the story is really "the best"). When students seem comfortable with the format, introduce another form. Continue this pattern throughout the year until students reach the point where they are completing and sharing different forms within their groups. And as always with such young students, provide a great deal of modeling, guidance, and assistance.

I think I can "train" my students well enough for them to be able to complete their role forms and share in their groups, but they just aren't ready for independent reading. What should I do?

The simple answer is to read the story or chapter aloud. Of course, this will limit students to using the same literature unless you have volunteers who can read different selections to other groups. Another option is to have students listen to recordings of literature (either prepared by you or professionally recorded) prior to completing their role forms and meeting in their groups.

I've explained the procedures to my class several times. I always have a few students who finish their role forms early and know where to go to wait for their group members, while half of the class seems lost and needs me to tell them when to finish and where to go! What should I do?

Ideally, you want to teach students the system and get them to the point where they are independent enough to do it all "on their own." However, when dealing with primary students, this is not always possible. A simple solution is to guide the class every step of the way, every time you do literature circles (or until they have progressed far enough to move on their own). By guiding students and regulating the time spent on each step, you will eliminate these problems. Eventually, students should be able to pace themselves and move from the reading to the role form completion to the group meeting to the whole class—all on their own.

Try this method of "time guidance." If students can complete the reading independently, circulate around the room throughout this step to ensure that they are about where they should be in order to finish the reading promptly. Help any students who need it and verbally alert students when reading time is almost up. (If the reading is being done in a read-aloud setting, this will not be an issue for you.) While students are completing their role forms, continue circulating around the room, assisting and encouraging the slower workers and slowing down the rushed ones. Tell students when there are only a few minutes left to complete their role forms. When you call time, direct students to their group meeting locations or simply have them sit in their groups from the beginning to avoid confusion. Tell students when to begin their discussions and continue to circulate. Remind students when there is a certain amount of time left and call time when appropriate. Bring students back together to do the whole-group wrap-up.

How can I occupy students who finish their reading or role forms faster than the rest of the class?

These "early birds" have a few options of what to do while waiting for the rest of their group members. (If your students are very young and have difficulty moving from one step to the other independently, you will guide them and keep track of time, so this will probably not be a problem for you. See previous question.) During this time, encourage students to do an activity related to the day's reading or current book. Familiarize students with whatever activity you choose before they begin so that they will not interrupt the rest of the class while trying to figure out what to do.

First, instruct students who finish early to gather their literature circle materials (books, pencils, and role forms) and go to their assigned group meeting locations. This signals to the other members that they are ready to begin discussing. Members who are still working on their role forms will make a mental note to speed up.

Next, as the early birds wait for their group members, they can reread the day's selection, read ahead, or review their role forms for errors or missing information. If you are working with an early chapter book, it may be difficult to stop students from reading ahead. Let them unless they are expected to make predictions as part of an assignment; students will benefit from reading the material more than once.

Also consider giving students the option of doing something extra, such as:
- highlighting vocabulary words in the books (or listing them on self-stick notes if the books do not belong to the students)
- marking interesting or favorite parts with self-stick notes
- responding to the reading in journals
- drawing their favorite parts or other aspects of the book
- writing letters to the author or characters from the book
- writing stories related to the book

How can I help a student who is slow to finish reading assignments or role forms?

It is normal and expected that students will take different amounts of time to finish the reading and their role forms. This is due not only to the differences in students' reading and writing abilities but also the differences in difficulty of the role forms (unless you are using the same role form for everyone). If a student is particularly slow at completing the role forms, first determine what is causing the delay. Is the student wasting time by being off task, or is he having trouble with the reading or role form? If the problem is caused by off-task behavior, use your normal management strategies to handle the situation. If the problem is due to the student's inability to work independently, pair him with a buddy or work one-on-one with him during the reading and role form completion time. Remember that the role forms can be adjusted for struggling students. Finally, if a student is not struggling but is just a slower reader or worker, consider allowing that student to complete a portion of each reading assignment or role form for homework.

I followed the steps in Chapter 3 to train my students, but they just don't seem to "get it." What else can I do to help them understand?

Don't give up! As stated in Chapter 3, expect to see some glitches early on. This type of interaction is probably new to young students, and they will need guidance and "training" for activities. The dialogue and discussion section is usually where primary students have the most difficulty. The first thing to do is observe and evaluate. Exactly what is it that students are not getting? Is it the steps involved? Is it the desired outcome? Is it the sharing time in the circles? Once you determine the areas where students need assistance, reteach these. It will be worth the extra time and effort required because once these students "get it," they will begin to function independently in their groups.

Many students have difficulty executing the discussions required in literature circles. Usually, the most effective way to handle this is to have students role-play the process again. You may decide to spend more time on this than you did in your original training sessions to ensure that students understand what is expected. Start by restating what should occur during the group time. Remind students that although they should share what is on their role forms, the goal of literature circles is to get them to talk about, discuss, and even debate the reading. Explain that these discussions should evolve naturally while they share their role forms and refer to the literature. Choose several student volunteers to role-play a literature circle meeting. Role-play along with students, perhaps serving as the Circle Supervisor, or have students role-play while you direct, guide, and provide specific feedback. Additionally, consider conducting a question-and-answer session to give students an opportunity to ask questions and clear up confusion. This will also help you determine what students do not understand about the process. Often this is all that it takes for students to get the hang of it. Finally, remember that they will get better with practice.

What can I do if students are just "skimming" rather than discussing the information on their role forms? How can I tell the difference?

Regardless of students' ages and abilities, you should still train them to discuss and share rather than to simply skim over the questions and answers on their role forms. Skimming most often occurs early on, when students are still not quite comfortable with the structure of literature circles. This also occurs with very young students who are still learning how to discuss and work cooperatively. The best way to handle this is to remind them that they should share their ideas, not just read their role form answers. Sitting in and participating with the groups also helps because you can lead the discussions. If the groups have already met a few times and they are still not discussing, take some time to reteach the concept. Explain what should occur during the group time and have students role-play the process again (see Chapter 3).

To give you an idea of the difference between skimming and discussing, here is an example of what a second-grade student who has completed a Bridge Builder form might say if he were skimming: "Here is what I drew. This is what I wrote . . ."

Here is an example of the same student using the Bridge Builder role form to initiate a discussion: "The story reminded me of a time when I was going to sleep over at my friend's house, and I was kind of scared. So, I drew myself at my cousin's house. See? That's my cousin, and that's me. I have my teddy bear in the picture, too, just like Ira in the book. I wrote that Ira reminded me of me when I was scared to sleep somewhere else, and my bear made me feel better, too. What about you?"

Of course, if the students are very young, their "discussions" will be much simpler, but that is okay. There is still a noticeable difference between skimming and sharing. Here is an example of an emerging reader who has completed the My Favorite Part role form and is only skimming: "I drew the part in the story when the caterpillar eats too much."

Here is an example of the same student using his role form to initiate a discussion "I drew the part in the story when the caterpillar eats too much. That was my favorite part because one time I ate too much candy, and I got a stomachache, too. What's your favorite part?"

How can I tell if a group is not working together effectively?

Sometimes there are obvious signs that a group is not working together well. This is especially the case with very young students who tend to tattle often and will definitely let you know if there are problems within the group. Although this will make it easy for you to figure out which groups are having difficulties, try to discourage students from doing this. Tattling goes against the spirit of cooperation that is critical for success with literature circles. Instead, remind students that the Circle Supervisor should help monitor the group and keep them focused. She is also the only one who may ask for teacher assistance during the actual circle time. If necessary, reteach the Circle Supervisor role.

Unfortunately, there are other times when the signs that a group is not working together well are not so clear. The following are signs to watch for that may indicate a lack of effectiveness and cooperation in a group:

- fights or arguments
- students' complaints to you
- groups who finish discussing significantly before the allotted time is up
- groups who do not finish discussing within the allotted time
- students' assessment worksheets that indicate problems
- one or more students who show reluctance to participate in literature circles (for example, asking to be excluded or moved to another group, preferring to work alone, or complaining regularly)

What can I do if a group is not working together effectively?

First, figure observe and monitor the group to figure out why the members are not working together effectively. Of course, if you sit in with the group, you may not see the problems that occur when you are not there. So, observe in a more subtle way, perhaps by sitting with a nearby group so that you can overhear and watch. Did students form this group? Is this perhaps a clique of friends that tend to bicker or socialize instead of work? Is one student causing the problem, or is it the dynamics of this particular group as a whole that just don't work?

Often when problems occur with the literature circles, it is because there is some uncertainty among the members about what they should do or say. This confusion can often lead to arguments. Therefore, it is imperative that you meet with the group in question and review the procedures, as well as try other strategies of reteaching.

If you have tried several strategies and the situation does not improve, you will have to decide whether to divide these group members and go through the trouble of reorganizing the groups. This depends on how long the groups have been meeting. If the best choice is to split up the group, it will be easier to do it early in the process than if the groups are midway through a book and have been meeting for

weeks. If students are near the end of a book, try to maintain the groups as they are and monitor this group more closely than the others by sitting with them more often or by recording their meetings when you are with other groups.

If all else fails, split up the group and have these students work independently on readings and role forms. Of course this is not ideal because the purpose of literature circles is for students to meet and discuss. Having them work independently means they will miss out on the most important component of the process. However, students who are denied the group-meeting experience even once usually want to return to their groups and will negotiate with you for another chance. As a teacher who wants students to benefit from this activity, you will be more than willing to come to an agreement!

I have a "problem student" who just isn't cooperating in the literature circle groups. I have tried everything! Should I exclude the student from the literature circles?

This is a difficult question but one most teachers have to answer at some point. Treat this like any other situation involving a "problem student." Every "problem student" is different and therefore warrants different considerations. You may have to adjust your expectations and goals for these students. Note that some of the young students will develop later in the year and will be able to show progress then.

With a first or second grader who should be able to participate fully, first assess whether you have really tried all options. Second, determine exactly how she isn't cooperating. Is she refusing to participate? If so, perhaps the student feels inadequate, unsure, or confused. Is she distracting other students in the group by the engaging them in off-task behaviors? If so, speak to the group members privately and ask them to ignore the problem student unless she is on task. Is she participating incorrectly by completing the role forms the wrong way, not following directions, or speaking out of turn? If so, perhaps she needs a review about appropriate literature circle participation. There are other general strategies you may want to try, as well. Consider assigning that student a "buddy" who will help her stay focused and on task. Work with the student one-on-one for a couple of weeks until you see some improvements. Have a private talk with the student to figure out why she is being uncooperative and brainstorm some possible solutions together. Write up a teacher-student contract about acceptable behaviors. Review the contract with the student and have her sign it.

If you have tried all of these things and nothing seems to work, then exclude the student from literature circles. This is especially important if she is constantly disrupting the rest of the class. Have the student do the same work as the rest of the class, except require her to do it independently

and without the opportunity of sharing with the group. Ideally, once the student has been excluded a couple of times, she will want to rejoin the group. When this occurs, allow her to return to the group under certain conditions and guidelines so that the disruptive behavior does not happen again.

How can I use literature circles for assessment purposes?

The work done in literature circles can be assessed for its own merit, or it can be used to assess a variety of skills. One easy way to assess skills is to take the time to create a rubric or checklist that includes the objectives you want students to master, such as comprehension, retelling, summarizing, vocabulary, etc., and then apply it to the role form that best demonstrates that skill. These rubrics will enable you to assess specific skills and learn about areas in which students need improvement and practice. For example, the Story Summarizer role forms are usually indicative of students' reading comprehension skills, so collect the Story Summarizer forms and compare them to your rubric. Assessment can focus on a particular role for each student, on all roles, or on the same role for each group, which would show how groups are performing on that skill.

Another type of assessment measures the cooperative behaviors exhibited in the circles. This might be especially useful for younger students who are still developing these social skills as required by most primary curriculums. Create rubrics for individual students or whole groups. These rubrics may measure very specific behaviors, such as "waits his turn." Or, use the assessment worksheets (pages 64–67) as guides. Fill out these forms while observing or participating during class time, or watching and listening to recorded group meetings. Along with student-completed assessment forms, this type of assessment can help you troubleshoot problems within groups and can indicate how to group students for the next book.

How do literature circles help students prepare for state tests?

Research proves that literature circles improve reading comprehension, a major component of many required tests. Literature circles give students opportunities to interact with literature and develop higher-order thinking skills. They must read independently or respond to text that is read aloud, then demonstrate evidence of comprehension by filling out role forms and participating in group meetings. The role forms cover general, critical elements of the study of literature and provide authentic opportunities to practice reading strategies. Students learn to recognize and apply these reading strategies and become more independent and active readers.

How can I prove to my principal/administrator that literature circles should be incorporated into my school curriculum?

There are several ways you can convince your principal that literature circles are an effective use of instructional time. First, research and provide hard evidence that literature circles are beneficial. (See Chapter 5 for a list of resources.) Another option is to invite the principal to observe literature circles in action. Surely, she will realize the advantages of literature circles once she sees motivated and

enthusiastic students reading, sharing, debating, interacting, and working. If inviting the principal to observe is not feasible, consider recording your students in their literature circles for the principal to watch and encourage her to ask questions and voice concerns. Once you have tried one or all of these tactics, your principal will probably see the benefits of literature circles.

How can I demonstrate literature circles to a group of parents or colleagues?

Usually, the most detailed and clear way to present literature circles to a group of adults is the same way that you present it to students, especially if the group is unfamiliar with the concept. However, you will rarely have time to get this intensive during a workshop. Regardless of your audience, the first step is to decide the purpose or goal of your presentation. Once you have identified the goal, the best means to present literature circles will be clear. Here are some general guidelines.

- If your goal is to motivate fellow teachers to implement literature circles in their own classrooms, one of the best ways to present the concept is to have them watch your students in action, either in person or on video.
- If your goal is to show parents what students do in class (for parents' night, for example), showing them a video of their children in their literature circle groups is also a great idea.
- If your goal is to show off your students to administrators or other visitors, have them observe your class during literature circle time.
- If your goal is to demonstrate to parents and fellow teachers (in a limited amount of time) how to implement literature circles, have them work in small groups to complete sample role forms using a literature excerpt from your class.

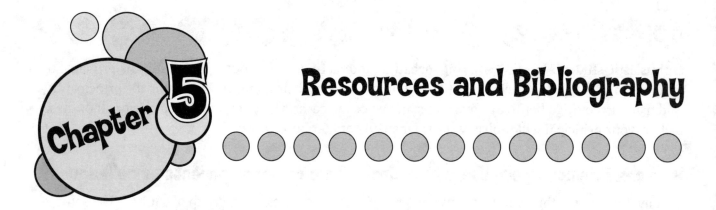

Resources and Bibliography

In the early 1980s, teachers like Karen Smith of Phoenix, Arizona helped start the literature circles "movement." Her students found a box of book sets, requested to borrow them, and formed their own book club discussions that were similar to book clubs for adults. Other teachers learned from these experiments that students function well when they choose their own literature and monitor their own progress.

Since literature circles began, many scholars have researched, studied, and implemented this approach to teaching literature. The concept has spread through presentations and articles by experts, theorists, and educators. The concept has also spread through the grassroots efforts of teachers who wanted to share with their colleagues this unique approach to teaching literature. Consult the following resources to learn more about the origins, benefits, and practices of literature circles.

Bibliography

Daniels, Harvey. *Literature Circles: Voice and Choice in the Student-Centered Classroom*. York, Maine: Stenhouse Publishers, 1994.

Hollingsworth, Liz. "Literature Circles Spark Interest." *Schools in the Middle* 8:2 (1998): 30-3.

Moen, Christine Boardman. *20 Reproducible Literature Circle Role Sheets: for Grades 1–3*. Carthage, Illinois: Teaching and Learning Company, 2000.

Rosenblatt, Louise. *The Reader, the Text, the Poem: The Transactional Theory of the Literary Work*. Carbondale, Illinois: Southern Illinois University Press, 1978.

Samway, Katharine Davies, and Gail Whang. *Literature Study Circles in a Multicultural Classroom*. York, Maine: Stenhouse Publishers, 1996.

Samway, Katharine Davies, G. Whang, C. Cade, M. Gamil, M. A. Lubandina, and K. Phommachanh. "Reading the Skeleton, the Heart, and the Brain of a Book: Students' Perspectives on Literature Study Circles." *The Reading Teacher* 45:3 (1991): 196-205.

Santa, Carol M., Lynn T. Havens, and Evelyn M. Maycumber. *Project CRISS: Creating Independence through Student-owned Strategies*. Dubuque, Iowa: Kendall Hunt Publishing Company, 1996.

Short, Kathy G., and Kathryn M. Pierce, Eds. *Talking about Books: Creating Literate Communities*. Portsmouth, New Hampshire: Heinemann, 1990.

Tompkins, Gail E. *50 Literacy Strategies: Step by Step*. Upper Saddle River, New Jersey: Prentice Hall, 2003.